PRAISE FOR *Finding US*

"*Finding US* is a book everyone will want to read. The why, when, and how to be the village for those braving mental illness. It is raw and honest. It includes tears, dreams, survival, hope, and a great deal of love."

Molly Fields
MN LPN Assoc. Board Director

"Reading Kristin's memoir is another reminder of the need we have to increase awareness and services for our mental health systems. Her message of unconditional love and acceptance of individuals living with mental illness is a message everyone can benefit from. I appreciate her courage to share her story (particularly as a mom also on a mental health journey with my son)."

Sarah Mason
Family Achievement Center President/Co-Owner
Family Achievement Foundation Board Chair/Founder

"Kristin, Anna and the entire Rehkamp family, thank you. Thank you for your vulnerability and courage to stand in the gap and share your story. You are a bright light of hope shining in the darkness for so many."

Lynn M. Moore MA, LADC, EAP
Founder, President - Acres for Life Therapy & Wellness

"Finding US illustrates the journey of courage, fear, frustration, joy, compassion, heartache, and love that is the experience of any family braving a pediatric mental health battle. As the parent of a child with severe anxiety, I can hear my own story in Kristin's words. She reminds us, even in the darkest days, no one is alone on this journey, and there is always reason to look ahead with hope."

Rachel Whitcomb
Mother; Wife; Vice President, Technology for a Fortune 100 Company

"A beautiful tribute to motherhood, vulnerability, and maintaining hope while facing the difficulty of an unknown path."

Amanda Jara
Director Clinical Performance, Bright Health

KRISTIN ROHMAN REHKAMP

Finding
US

A MOTHER'S MEMOIR OF
BRAVING MENTAL ILLNESS
WITH HER
YOUNG DAUGHTER

atmosphere press

To my husband — you are my hero.

To my children — always be strong and brave.

To my parents — thank you for the courage.

AUTHOR'S NOTE

Living with a mental illness is a journey (rarely, if ever, a linear process) that is messy, complicated, and often misunderstood — readers may notice this in my writing. An experience, however (despite our best efforts), we cannot control, but instead bravely learn to live with, learn from, and feasibly teach others around us along the way.

Our family purposefully shares our story to educate and bring visibility to what living with a child braving a mental illness looks like and feels like. We have found there is a fair amount of information available about what a mental illness is, its symptoms, and even how you might approach treatment. There is very little available about the emotional impact or how it feels for the family/friends/community living with and supporting a loved one courageously battling mental illness. We invite you into the fold of our experience (week by week, chapter by chapter) to educate, reduce stigmas, and decrease unknowns that might form the wrong assumptions and even create apprehension and fear.

When we are sick (let's say a "cold"), we are the same person...we simply do not feel good and might behave differently (more sleep, lots of tissues for our runny nose, inability to work or go to school, headache...etc.). Living with a mental illness is no different. These individuals are still themselves (personality, aspirations, and goals) ...they simply do not feel well and behave differently. We need to always take care to love them as they are and meet them where they might be.

We are hopeful our family and story help normalize the mental health conversation while at the same time providing others with a similar experience, comfort, and support in knowing we understand your unique challenges — we understand you and your journey. Find peace and strength by simply knowing you are not alone.

INTRODUCTION

My name is Kristin. Proud mother to a beautiful 13-year-old girl that experienced an unexpected and alarming panic attack at her 11-year-old well-child check on September 16, 2020, that triggered an acute anxiety/severe panic disorder (a Mayo diagnosis, not mine) that changed our life, perspective, and path forward suddenly and without warning. Any stigmas or preconceived ideas about mental illness...let's just get rid of those right now. Our daughter is blessed with a loving family, beautiful home, and safe community of friends and neighbors. She's an A-student and a dancer. Sadly, like any physical illness, mental illness can present just as suddenly and happen to any of us.

Prior to September 16, 2020, our daughter had no indicators of any underlying mental health conditions or illness. Our daughter's sensory system, following her first and only panic attack, never relented and got progressively worse. Symptoms included fluttering/upset stomach, dizziness, feelings of being hot, racing heart, perceived shortness of breath, and loss of sensation in limbs. Her panic attacks or irrational state of fear could/can last minutes or hours, often appearing seizure-like (uncontrollable body movements, disassociation, and sometimes an inability to speak). She enters a state of fight-or-flight...and WILL fight (aggression both verbal and physical) and WILL flee...we have found her hiding in unusual places (once under our snowblower in the garage) and trying to leave the house (a couple of times in her PJs in sub-zero temps). Our daughter often mentions "life does not feel real," and dying feels easier.

In less than two weeks after that first panic attack at a routine well-child check, our daughter was admitted to a local hospital and, for seven days, waited for an inpatient mental health bed. Her symptoms got progressively worse...terrifyingly worse... nearly resulting in sedation and restraint to calm her body, mind, and sensory system that was malfunctioning. From that moment on, our daughter was in-and-out of mental health hospitals for nearly two months and on various different psychotropic drugs that did not appear to do her any favors (despite best intentions). Medications made her feel worse (specifically increasing dizziness), and the induced physical symptoms associated with panic scared her... increasing her anxiety. It became a vicious cycle. The sicker our daughter felt...the greater her anxiety, and the more severe and often her panic presented. Her world became very small. She was unable to attend 6th grade or dance with her team. We could not attend the children's museum or the zoo for more than 45 minutes. A hot boat ride, cold water swim, or go-kart race tripped physical symptoms resulting in panic attacks. She survived in a protective bubble..."living" was paused.

It quickly became painfully obvious that mental illness does not just impact one person. It impacts a family...a community. There were times my husband and I had to ask our nine-year-old son to take his five-year-old sister into her bedroom. He knew to grab a movie and headphones and to close the door to avoid the unwelcome sounds and sights of the panic attacks that plagued our oldest. I cannot begin to describe how that felt as a parent recognizing the insanity of the ask and the horrible reason for the ask.

In addition, I remember tears from our littlest every time we took her sister to a medical appointment. Tears that stemmed from our eldest's second ER visit resulting in a transfer to a local inpatient mental health hospital. Our littlest never got to say "goodbye" to her older sister and waited seventeen days to see her again. Every time our oldest experienced a panic attack, it induced fear in our littlest around the possibility that her sister would be "taken" and not come home. I remember being in the throes of keeping our oldest daughter safe while my heart broke for our other two children, lost in the chaos of it all. Experiencing things...being asked to do things...seeing and hearing things you would never wish for any child.

Between September 2020 and August 2021, we logged a total of three ER visits, three extended hospital stays, and a trip to Mayo. We have a medical 3-ring binder for our daughter that is bursting at the seams. In February 2021, I put my corporate career on hold...adding care provider to my personal/professional resume. I remind myself every day that my greatest and most important job is and always will be "mom." The job does not come with a fancy corporate title like those I have held in the past or a paycheck that supported a more than comfortable lifestyle. I have neither of those today...but I have our daughter.

We slowly move forward. Day-by-day. Along the way, we take some right turns, and we take some wrong turns. But we have learned and continue to learn. We learn about our daughter, we learn about mental illness, and we learn how to be a support system and stronger for each other.

I read the book *Limitless* by Mallory Weggemann (a Paralympic gold medalist). Her words resonate deeply and often occupy my thoughts.

Mallory wisely says, "Life is about the long game, and what seems overwhelming in the moment could very well be pointing us toward something greater. It's up to us to push past the noise of our present, past expectations placed upon us, and into the boundless possibilities of our unwritten future."

From Mallory and others in my life who quietly and patiently guide, coach, and love me, I am learning that there isn't really such a thing as going back to "normal" after trauma or tragedy. You cannot go back because somewhere along the way, your perception of normal changes based on your experience. Life for me...for our daughter...for our family...is still limitless. It will just be different.

Although I may never understand the "why" behind our journey with our daughter, I do believe all things happen for a reason. I am hopeful our family will lend a strong and positive voice for children/adolescents, families, and those serving our communities working to break down barriers, raise awareness and make a difference in the lives of those braving mental illness. As we advocate for our daughter, we look forward to evolving mental health/well-being thinking and care models for those that journey with us. These individuals and families are some of the most courageous people we know.

I look forward to tomorrow without the fear and uncertainty the past has caused, realizing the blessings and strength that have found us when not looking. Life marches on...it always will. We cannot control the deck we are dealt, but we do get to choose how we play the cards. Remember... we are playing the long game. Life always goes on...and so must we.

Continue living.

I WILL NEVER FORGET

We were terrified we were going to lose her. Our daughter was waking up and going to sleep in a panic or state of fight-or-flight...she felt like she could not breathe, her chest hurt, loss of sensation in limbs, dizziness, disorientation, headaches...all rolling up to a state of terror I had never in my life witnessed. Our daughter thought she was dying...and if that was not bad enough...she preferred dying over the way she was feeling. Regardless if her symptoms were perceived (symptoms of anxiety and panic) or real...it was her reality. There was/is no comfort in knowing they were not "real"...not for her...not for us.

Hospitals/ERs are not always equipped to handle a mental health crisis...yet the only place for those with a mental health crisis to go—a result of the "system"...not a choice.

I will forever be grateful for the compassionate team at the children's hospital that cared for our daughter. However, they did not specialize in children's mental illness. Their role was simply to prevent self-harm while we waited...and waited. Our daughter kept shouting, "Why aren't you doing anything? Why is no one doing anything?" She was right...absolutely right...no one was attempting a diagnosis or treatment...the team's primary and only role was to keep her safe by not allowing her to leave the hospital room or even use the bathroom alone. We waited and prayed we would get her transferred to a mental health hospital before we needed to sedate and restrain her...and so you can understand and feel the weight of this unfathomable idea...our daughter was an eighty-pound eleven-year-old girl that still believed in fairies and holiday magic.

On Monday (October 5, 2020), we learned our daughter's case had been reviewed and approved for admission into a local inpatient mental health hospital. This after spending seven days in the hospital...like so many others, we waited in fear and prayed for a miracle...still trying to grasp that just two weeks earlier, our daughter was living her life with no indication of a mental illness.

Our oldest (who was transferred by ambulance) was accepted via patient intake (alone). My husband and I walked through the front doors (without our daughter) after driving separately (per policy — not our choice). Emotionally and physically exhausted, we learned only one of us could see her at a time (leaning on each other was not an option). I removed electronics from my person, walked through a metal detector, and was escorted down a long hallway by security. Nothing about this experience felt comfortable.

I was taken to room #8, the last door on the right. The door was unlocked by staff, and I found our daughter alone, scared and crying...in new hospital garments I did not recognize. For safety reasons, the room was simple...and sterile. A small bed with a blanket. Wood desk and nightstand. Hard floors and walls. Small bathroom with a soft door to discourage any self-harm. Windows were frosted — you could not see out (intended to protect patient privacy).

Independently, my husband and I each had 5 minutes to say "goodbye" to our daughter, who desperately begged us not to leave her. With broken hearts, we left the hospital not fully comprehending what just happened...sense of control over the situation lost. There is nothing...absolutely nothing...that pre-pares you for a moment like this. And yet, I still remember the weight of knowing that because our daughter got a bed at a children's mental health hospital, another child still waited.

THE TOUGHEST SOLDIERS ARE GIVEN THE HARDEST MISSIONS

So, how do you parent a child that has lived a pretty blessed life with no reason to fear or not to believe in the "happy ending" (now I am asked all the time, "Why me?" and "Am I going to die?") How do you parent this sudden and new reality? Again, our daughter went into a routine well-child check as the girl we once knew but left her appointment on the verge of an acute panic disorder she now battles every day.

Well, there once again is no magic manual for parenting in this situation (if anyone finds that darn manual, will you let me know?) I can assure you without a doubt that we make a lot of mistakes, trying our very best to do the right thing. I wish we could do some things over in our attempts to help our daughter, but many remind me we can only go forward.

For reference and education...panic attacks can last minutes or hours. A person goes into an irrational state of fear that, in some cases, can appear seizure-like (uncontrollable body movements, disassociation, and sometimes an inability to speak). They enter a state of fight-or-flight...and WILL fight (aggression both verbal and physical) and WILL flee...we have found our daughter hiding in unusual places (once under our snowblower in the garage) and trying to leave the house (a couple of times in her PJs in sub-zero temps). Our daughter often mentions "life does not feel real," her heart hurts, chest hurts, she cannot breathe, dizziness, loss of sensation in limbs, tingling sensation in hands/feet, and a feeling of being "hot." Regardless if symptoms are real, they are her reality and feel VERY real to her.

Sometimes a panic attack can start or look like a temper tantrum, and that is where the confusion lies. How you parent a temper tantrum and a panic attack are very different, but as parents, we have only had experience parenting a temper tantrum. We often have to remind ourselves that we cannot rationalize with a person who is currently irrational, given brain functions that have momentarily gone off-line. Our daughter has taught us. She often reminds us to be kind, soft, quiet, and patient. Once again, I am reminded of how much she is teaching us every day...and not just for her, but for so many others.

So, there is the acute anxiety and panic attacks, but there is also "loss." Our daughter misses school, her dance team dances without her, she lost innocence (sadly witnessed a child trying to commit suicide during a hospital stay), and she simply does not feel good, so everything she does takes a bit more energy and is never certain. How do I protect her from the downstream impacts or effects of all of this?

After our daughter came home from one of her hospital stays, she put a note on my desk. It read, "God gives the toughest soldiers the hardest missions." Our daughter reminds me every day how tough and special she is. I remind her she is meant to be and do something EVEN greater than before. I still have this little note on my bulletin board in my office. It helps me/us accept where we are at and look forward to tomorrow.

ACCEPT THIS MOMENT
AND FIND PEACE

I have had a hard day. It should not have been a hard day and probably really wasn't. Some days just feel easier than others... maybe I am reminded more on some days than others that things are different than they were at this same time last year.

The day started out with the planning and execution of a birthday party for our golden retriever, Finnley. There were homemade doggie cupcakes (which I learned later both the children and dogs ate — oh boy), treat bags, streamers, balloons, and gifts (from the neighbor dogs, of course). At one point, there were seven kids and four dogs in our garage...yep, chaos and lots of barking!

While the kids played and the dogs barked (and I prayed all were accounted for), I spent the afternoon connecting with our daughter's medical team, our mental health case manager, various school partners, and later in the day, her dance studio.

But, truth be told, I wish our daughter did not need a "team." I do not want to spend my afternoons and evenings on the phone or writing emails advocating for her. I want to be in the garage playing with our children. Reading a book just for fun. A run around the trails of Lake Elmo or a glass of wine on the porch. Anything, but being reminded that things are different. That life for all of us is different.

Our life bounces between crisis and survival...today and tomorrow. Today I struggle to know how to get our daughter to "tomorrow" because she has been so protected or guarded. How we care for her and support her has to evolve with her. She needs to know life as she knew it still exists with all the same opportunities as her peer group or what existed prior to September 16, 2020. She does not want to be forgotten, lost in the shuffle, or to be treated differently...yet she is. And my hope is someday, our daughter sees how wonderfully different, strong, and special she truly is.

Every day I remind myself to accept this moment and find peace in it. My day was hard, and life is different. But I remind myself there are many, many "good" different things too.

YOU HAVE THE POWER TO MOVE THE UNIVERSE IN THE DIRECTION OF BEAUTY

So yesterday, our oldest daughter was putting on her shoes and heading to the mailbox. I asked her, "What are you doing, honey?"

She responds, "I am mailing a letter to the president."

I paused. "Ahh, what is the letter about, and where did you find an address?"

She says matter-of-factly, "I googled it." (An obvious response, but one has to admire the gumption.)

And she continues, "The letter is asking all responding in a crisis (first responders, moms and dads, people on the street) to be kind and compassionate." She goes on to say, "If an individual is living with a mental illness, a high stress situation makes it worse. These individuals are misunderstood and only trying to do the right thing with an illness that can be disabling. They wish they were not sick and are probably doing the best they can."

Pretty powerful letter and reminder from an eleven-year-old girl. She is obviously paying attention to the world around her and weaving her story through it. Although you might think I give her strength and courage (I am "mom"), it is our daughter who inspires me every day with her courage and tenacity. She reminds me often that we all have the power to move the universe in the direction of beauty.

"I AM A SURVIVOR."

Let me introduce you to our youngest daughter. She is our five-year-old. Our beautiful blonde, curly-haired free-spirit. We call her our little spitfire...never afraid, always curious, and quite hilarious. Because of her cute little personality (and ability to get away with just about anything), she has had a pretty blessed little life. People seem to gravitate to her naturally and easily; therefore, she is always happy and entertaining.

My mom came down for a visit the other day. I heard her enter the house and have a conversation with our littlest (still in her PJs and hair tossed all about). My mom (or grandma) says, "Hi, honey. How are you this morning?" Without missing a beat, our little girl responds, "I am a survivor, Grandma, I am a survivor."

To this day, I am not sure our littlest understood what she said. But the funny thing is...what a spot-on remark... appropriate for any of us who lived a year with Covid, but especially for a little girl who has watched her older sister battle a mental illness for days and months.

There have been times this little girl watched her big sister leave the house and not come home for nearly three weeks after an extended hospital stay that started with an ER visit.

Let alone not understanding the "why" and "what" with her sister, she often did not get to say, "Goodbye, I love you, and when will you be home?" She has watched her big sister (who she adores and looks up to) disappear, not want to play or talk, hit, scream, and run away from home. And again, this all happened overnight, so for this little girl, a change none of us understood or could explain to her. Today she is watching her older sister slowly return...with good days and bad days, so nothing is consistent, predictable, or at times, makes sense. Sadly, we watch our littlest change in her efforts to protect and care for her older sister. A bit less delightfully carefree and significantly more worried.

Mental illness does not just impact one person. It impacts a family...a community. It is not just "one" that needs support, understanding, and healing...it is many. It even impacts our hilarious, happy-go-lucky little girl that should not have a care in the world...but sadly does.

"JUST HIT THE DARN BALL"

In just a few days, our daughter will be front and center. She will be dancing at her first dance competition in a long time, 2nd ever and 1st solo...her only dance this year as a result of her illness and ongoing hospitalization. She will walk on stage and perform her solo (Alicia Keys, "Back to Life" — purposefully chosen).

Sadly, our daughter has had panic attacks at her last two solo practices and has not danced much in the last few weeks, yet is competing against girls that are dancing 8 hours a week. My natural instinct as a mom is to protect her. We suggested she compete at a level lower (we wanted her to have and feel success). We offered her the opportunity to wait another month to get and feel stronger.

I learned a powerful lesson this week. Our daughter's panic was not out of fear — fear of failure, forgetting her dance, or having a panic attack on the stage and running off. I learned those fears were mine and mine alone. I assumed that our daughter shared the same fears, and I was protecting her by offering her alternatives. Our daughter does not have reservations about being on stage or failure. Instead, she did not understand why we did not believe she could do it when she believed she could. Darn it...I got that one all wrong. I then told our daughter a story....

I grew up an avid tennis player. My parents invested a lot of time and money to give me every opportunity to play and be great (private lessons, camps, and tournaments). During my senior year, I "got into my head" (believing and terrified I was letting everyone down) and could no longer hit the ball. I had a horrible season and watched my tennis career slowly come to an abrupt end. I still remember the moment (30 years later) — that cognitive decision to simply "hit the darn ball" — what did I have to lose? But I did know...I had a lot to gain... and not a medal, but a sense of pride and accomplishment. I hit the ball over and over...and eventually made it to the Minnesota State Tennis Tournament. I learned I was letting no one down. Instead, they wanted to protect me, but I needed them to believe in me.

I told our daughter to get on that stage Saturday and "just hit the darn ball!" I am going to stop protecting her and start empowering her. I suspect it might be hard, but what do we have to lose? Instead, I focus on how much we have to gain.

THIS, RIGHT HERE, IS SPECIAL

I write this entry to our daughter. She took the stage recently at a dance competition for the first time in over a year post-trauma. She did it feeling anxious, dizzy, and nauseous (her meds and illness at play on top of your typical nerves before any competition)...but she also did it with courage, determination, and grace.

Dear Daughter,

I reflect back to September and our time in the hospital. How scared (terrified) and confused we all were. What was happening? Who could help? Why was no one helping...or fast enough? I remember the terror in your eyes — a look I had never seen before...gut-wrenching for a parent. I remember feeling helpless and mad at the world. Why our daughter? And why you...you are such a beautiful soul. I remember hospital personnel suggesting sedation and restraint. I remember calling everyone I knew, begging for help. You had told us you wanted to die. Not because you did not like your life, but because you did not want to live "this way." We promised to "make it better." A promise your dad and I hoped we could keep.

We slowly moved forward...very slowly. Day-by-day. We take some right turns, and we have taken some wrong turns, but we learn. We learn about you, we learn about your illness, we learn how to be a support system and stronger for each other. We cry a lot. We also laugh a lot and reflect on our blessings. Your dad always says the one certainty we have every day..."the sun always comes up." We clung to this..., hoping the next day would bring us a miracle or a sense of peace and calm during times when your panic was at its worst.

Never in my life have I been prouder of something or someone. Never. You took the stage and looked so beautiful. And although, yes, you were donned in a lot of glitz and glam, that is not what was beautiful. For the first time in a long time, I saw "you." I saw your light. Your eyes danced, and you were all smiles. You were truly happy and at peace on that stage. I cried.

I will never forget those 2 mins and 14 seconds...never. You sparkled in every way. I am so proud of you! You have shown me what courage truly is, and I could not be more grateful for this special and powerful bit of knowledge. I hope you hold on to that moment on the stage and cherish it. It will be your superpower...a power you can use in the future when extra courage and faith are needed. But like any hero with a super-power, I hope you share it with others and use it only for good. Remember to thank and appreciate all those that help you be "super."

I always thought and hoped you could get on that stage yesterday. I think you always knew you could...you needed to show me. Now we both know you can.

Love,
Mom

THERE IS NO
"ONE RIGHT WAY" TO BE

Our daughter lives with anxiety...we watch it. Most of us know it as a feeling of being stressed or nervous. For our daughter...we watch it consume and control her. Almost like a second personality that sometimes decides what kind of day she is going to have (happy, sad, easy, or hard), how she will feel, how she will act, and even how she might treat others. She is not always even aware of or in control of her emotions and actions. And...anytime we are making medication adjustments ...it is even worse. Doctors refer to the change in behavior as the "black box label warning"—increased anxiety, increased depression, increased suicidal thoughts, increased panic... basically...it spells "not fun." We often wonder if it is worth it.

Our daughter conquered her dance competition. And even more important — she felt like she was a part of the team again — even if just for a moment. She was herself or as close to herself as we had seen in months. The fairytale crashed on Monday. Enter "reality" and a med change (note black box warning above). Sadly, we have two med changes over the next 4 weeks, so the month ahead will be tough. While our daughter's peers might be looking forward to the upcoming dance competitions, end of the school year, and the promise of warmer weather, our daughter is looking forward to being past medication changes that make her feel sick and not act like herself.

Our daughter did not place in the Top 5 Overalls for her solo...her hope...the rest of us were still celebrating her victory of simply getting on the stage this past weekend. Although our daughter recognized the accomplishment...what was our goal...was not hers. She still holds onto who she was and the potential of who she can be. The hard part as a child and parent...right now (present-day) is different.

I sat in the back of the studio celebration. I was not like the other moms in the audience who were there to simply celebrate their children. I was there to celebrate our daughter but also as a care provider. I had a few minutes to be just "mom" until our daughter started crashing in the front row of 30 dancers when she realized she had not placed. I do not believe her change in emotion was about placing. This may be what others saw and even what her words reflected. But instead, I believe it was the sudden reality or consequence of being sick and not being physically and mentally able to dance as much as her peers. I watched her anxiety start to consume her, and panic setting in, illustrated by rocking and trembling. I watched as her friends tried to console her, and hurt set in as they realized there was nothing they could do. I had to remove our daughter from the studio. What is worse for an 11-year-old girl — your mom removing you from a public setting or having a public panic attack?

Our daughter cried...in the car on the way...at home. Really, really cried. We just let her be with her sadness and loss (and I mean the last six months and life as we know it now). We told her to be sad and mad tonight, but tomorrow she had a choice. She could either give up or continue to fight. One is certainly easier than the other, but I hope she continues to fight and realizes along the way that there is no "one right way" to be, but it can be just as beautiful and amazing!

"WHY FIT IN WHEN YOU WERE BORN TO STAND OUT?"
– Dr. Seuss

I am going to keep this one short and sweet. I am wrapped in a blanket by the fireplace, enjoying a quiet house and a glass of red wine. A rare moment for a family of five. A moment I am cherishing.

Reflecting on our week...it was a hard one. Activities such as folding a load of laundry, attending a dance class, or finishing a school assignment used to be so simple and often taken for granted (because they were so simple). Now, such events are an accomplishment and something we celebrate.

I cannot help but wonder (like our daughter or others that might walk in our shoes), "Why?" — "Why us?" and "How Come?" We may never understand the "why" or "how come," ....but we can embrace it. (And "we" is me, my husband, our daughter, our other two children, family, friends, and everyone else reading this book right now that is journeying alongside us.) Often, I want to be mad at the world, curl up in a ball, and pull the sheets over my head. And many have told me I deserve to feel this way and even tried to convince me TO feel this way. BUT, being mad and sad will not get me anywhere, and certainly not make me a productive and positive role model for our children.

I was reminded of a Dr. Seuss quote I often reflect on when struggling to be at peace and meet our daughter where she is at. The quote is, "Why fit in when you were born to stand out?" Our daughter reminds us every day that instead of being sick...she is special. Instead of being just like everyone else... she is not. Instead of following others...she is paving her own way. I can be mad...I can be sad...or I can be thankful. Thankful for lessons that remind us what is really important and gratitude (not just the gratitude we say, but the gratitude we feel).

IT DOESN'T GET EASIER,
BUT YOU GET STRONGER

Yesterday was a hard day, and I am still reeling. On the outside, no one would know...we, our home, our life looks pretty "normal" (air quotes because really — what is normal, anyway?). On the inside, I am sad, scared, and uncertain. The bad moments (although less than the good) are a painful reminder that our life is different and our child is sick. This is hard (not going to sugar coat it)....especially when you compare or watch others live the life you used to have.

Yesterday and last Monday, our daughter had pretty severe panic attacks leaving a counseling session. Unfortunately, these panic attacks happened in the car, which was (and still is) both difficult and dangerous for my daughter and me. You have to remember panic attacks are a state of irrational fear, and the body automatically goes into a state of fight-or-flight (most often uncontrollable). If an attack happens in the car, our daughter wants to flee the car or "run away from" — a natural response to something that is causing fear or pain. However, for the parent or care provider driving the car, pulling over or stopping is not always in the best interest of the driver and child.

We pulled over once out of concern for the safety of our

other two children in the car, but quickly realized we just let a child in an irrational state of fear run from the car...how were we going to get her back in the car and would she run into traffic or simply run away? Thankfully, in that situation, I had my husband to help me. Yesterday and last Monday, it was just me.

I did not know then and still do not know today the right decision, but instinct tells me to get my daughter and myself to a safe place. So, yesterday and last Monday, I drove with my arm held like a barrier between her and me for protection. Our daughter screamed, hit the car, hit me, bit me, yelled and screamed out the window, "someone help me," and grabbed the steering wheel at 55 mph a couple of times in an attempt to pull the car over. When stopped at a light and your daughter is pounding windows with her fists, hitting the dashboard with her feet, and screaming for help out the window, it is difficult not to feel judged and fear a potential intervention if the situation was misread.

So...with this context...

...please do not judge me for not pulling over. A parked car at the side of a highway in the middle of nowhere with a panicked child could result in an irreversible accident involving my child and others. I could never forgive myself.

...please do not judge me for keeping her home when she should be in school. Trust me, the lost time has broken our hearts and scares our daughter. We are doing everything we can to get her back to school.

...please do not judge me for allowing her to compete in her dance competitions even though she is not attending dance classes. I cannot count all the tears in an effort to get her to class, the number of notes to her teachers, or how many times we have sat in the car or in the lobby...just steps away. I do not understand why she can compete and why classes are causing panic attacks. You have no idea how much I wish I understood, to help our daughter and to explain it to others.

Trust that we re-evaluate every day.

...please do not judge me if I think I can safely put her on an airplane to see her cousins in CO (her birthday wish). My brother is a nurse, and we are staying at his home. But, a trip to Texas for Dance Nationals may not be feasible because we would not be in a safe place with family and in a very public setting (hotel and convention center). Again, intervention can be both welcomed and terrifying. I realize none of this is very rational or makes much sense...trust me...I know

...please do not judge me or others for not knowing how to parent a mentally ill child. Each day there are new hurdles and uncertainty. I am not sure if it gets easier or if one gets stronger. I have to believe and hold on to the faith that sooner or later...I will be stronger...and it might even get just a little easier. Trust all the other families supporting a child (young or older) braving a mental illness might say the same thing and always assume good intent. Please lead with care and compassion...do not be quick to judge.

RIGHT NOW, YOU ARE PERFECT

A note to our daughter...

Happy 12th birthday, honey! Today friends and family will celebrate you and the beautiful person you are.

This morning we were snuggling, and you said, half asleep, "Mom, I do not tell you this enough, but thank you." I am reminded on so many occasions what a special person you are.

I still remember when you were born. It was an unusually warm May...the tulips were in full bloom...I remember thunderstorms. You graced the world at 1 pm on Monday, May 4th, 2009...just a day after our first wedding anniversary...you were a bit of a sweet surprise. You were a small (but perfect) little thing (even at full-term), weighing 6 lbs. and 13 ounces. You were born with blue eyes and dark curly hair (that would eventually turn blonde). I recall we started calling you our little bear in the hospital...a nickname of endearment...we still call you bear today...we call you our brave bear.

Like most parents, we wish only the best for you. We hope for happiness and love. We pray you find peace in your journey and people along the way that will love and accept you just as you are. Chase all your dreams without reservation or fear...be sure to extend gratitude to all who help you along the way.

Never take anyone for granted. Remember to say "thank you." Do something bigger than you...put others first, and give back where you can. You are a kind soul...you always have been... never lose this wonderful quality. As simple as it may be, it just might be your superpower in our world today.

Today, dreams might feel like they have changed or feel far away. I know, honey...I know. This week (your birthday week) you have gene testing, hormone testing, a physical, bloodwork, vital check, two sessions of counseling, a neuropsychological exam, and an EEG. Gratefully, these tests and appointments are much less invasive than those of the past. I guess we should be thankful for that...but it is okay to be sad/mad too. I know I am sometimes.

We will get past all of this...you are strong and brave. And when I say "get past,"...I recognize it may be something we live with, but I have all the confidence we will figure out "how" to live with it...and not just live, but flourish and grow. I believe in my heart of hearts that you were chosen by angels to be bigger than you are. When you believe all things happen for a reason and have faith in this idea, it does make things easier...so I believe...I hope you do, too. Before we know it, you will be talking about prom (gosh, help us!), high school gradu- ation, and adventures you will embark on. I have all the confidence you will be as amazing as you are today.

I need you to know...I need you to believe with all your heart...that right now, you are perfect. Regardless if we under- stand or will ever understand why you are taking the road less traveled, you are who you are meant to be, and I am confident your journey will be beautiful. I need you to be strong and have confidence there is a plan for you much bigger than most. When days or moments are hard..."believe"...it is my birthday wish for you.

Love you,
Mom

REFLECT ON THREE THINGS YOU ARE GRATEFUL FOR

"Reflect on Three Things You are Grateful For" ...I know how I **would have** answered that before our daughter got sick...and without pause...my job/career, my husband/family, and our health. Two of three are very much still true today. But, as I sit here and reflect on our oldest daughter's mid-week dance competition and our youngest daughter's surgery today, I realize that there was a time in my life...my professional career...that I would have been unable to attend one or both (and if the inability to attend was reality, perception or guilt... decision or outcome would have been the same). A time in my life when I identified myself by what I did and not by who I was or what I valued. And if I had attended...I know I would not have been present...buried in emails, phone calls, and trying to be important. Many others balance mom and career better than I...I was, quite frankly...horrible at it.

So today...at a much different time in my life, I reflect very differently on "Three Things I am Most Grateful For," and realize again that our oldest daughter's journey has quietly re-centered our lives and priorities in the background of a year full of challenges.

I am grateful to be present in our children's lives. I make our children breakfast before school (eggs, waffles, pancakes, sausage). I know our son read his essay to his class yesterday. I know our daughter rode a horse named "Pepper" during her riding lesson. I know our youngest had two blue popsicles at the hospital, followed by a bag of goldfish. I know our son and his grandpa rode bikes yesterday afternoon, stopping for an ice cream cone along the way. I know our oldest daughter made homemade bread with her grandma. Our son made a solar system at Cub Scouts, and our littlest and I snuggled before bed. There was a time in my life when these simple observations/ activities would have been peripheral to my career and other demands on my time...I am grateful they are now front-and-center.

I am grateful for a greater sense of peace and calm. Anyone who knows me or our busy family would argue the idea of "peace" within ten miles of our house. I might tend to agree, so I better elaborate. I am at peace knowing what is really important to our family and finally putting these values ahead of careers/personal aspirations and the golden hand-cuffs we may have been bound by. Instead of trying to fit our family into our careers and a lifestyle, we are now designing our life and careers around our family...even integrating them. And not just talking...finally doing. Interesting that feeling like we had nothing to lose forced a changed hand...and honestly...if we had not changed... everything we had would have been lost.

I am grateful to know who I am and the legacy I will leave our children. Pivoting your life is terrifying...especially with the unknowns of a child braving a mental illness. But more than any other time in my life, I am confident in who I am and the legacy I will leave our children. I hope our children will remember "mom" being home as I remember my mom being home and the sense of stability it provided. I will forever cherish the opportunity to be our oldest daughter's care provider...there is so much beauty to be found even in some of the darkest moments. I hope our children might truly understand and appreciate the opportunity to be a voice and influence on the stigmas of mental illness....that someday a child, adolescent, family, or individual might benefit from our story. I hope they lead with empathy, kindness, and compassion recognizing differences might simply need to be better heard and understood. The legacy we leave our children will not be grandiose, but I am hopeful the simplicity of living a life full of happiness, love, and servitude is someday recognized as an even greater gift.

BE YOUR OWN HERO TODAY

On a day we celebrate mothers, I reflect on what "mom" really means. And for me, this year (like so many others), this job description has changed. I hope all moms find some peace today, knowing...quite frankly...that we have all been super-heroes and absolutely deserve some grace and a pedicure!

This year I have had to add caregiver to my "mom" resume. Caregiver is not a job description any mom ever wants to see on her resume. And with caregiver, you are also a care manager, care coordinator, administer of care, advocate for your child/family, and sometimes a down and dirty fighter in a healthcare system that can sometimes be so difficult and frustrating to navigate.

I was a kindergarten teacher this year...gosh, our poor littlest. Back when one chooses a career...I purposefully chose not to be a teacher because I know patience is not my virtue (it does not even hit the list of "maybes"). But I had no choice, like so many other moms/parents this year. So, I put on my big girl pants, pulled out the "snap words," and got to it! Our littlest read me a book last night, and I was so proud of her...and a bit proud of me. Thank goodness I had not completely failed her.

I now serve and advocate for an area of health or medicine

that is misunderstood and not well understood. Like so many others in our world that are seemingly "okay" most of the time, so is our oldest daughter. She is a beautiful, kind, compassionate soul who only and truly wants to be and do good. But yesterday, if you were one of five that walked off the elevator at her pediatric clinic and found our twelve-year-old daughter screaming hateful words and hiding under a 3-foot wide bench...assumption naturally is she might be a troubled child versus a sick child. Maybe that I am a horrible mom... versus a mom standing by and protecting our daughter from harm while I wait for her brain to come back online. How many other moms are doing the same and praying their child (young or older) gets help before it is too late and we do not misjudge, label, or give up on them?

I am now a stay-at-home mom. No longer a vice president or director in Fortune 500 businesses. Instead, I run a home and a team of five with my husband. I traded in my suits for yoga pants, my outlook calendar for school calendars, my corporate happy hours for after-school snacks, and my cleaning help for a bucket of Lysol. Without a doubt, this is the harder job....and not nearly as glamorous. Someday I will do my hair again and maybe even wear make-up...someday.

I am a protector...sadly...when did I need to become a protector?! I protect our children from illness, social media, politics, and social unrest...in addition to...looking both ways before crossing the street. I have no idea how to navigate this new space and while doing so...assure our children do not grow up in fear but instead hopeful and with faith in good and people.

I am Kristin. Daughter to two amazing parents who always have and continue to be my guiding lights, my role models, and my strength. I am sister to an amazing younger brother I have always admired for what he does, but more importantly...for who he is. I am a wife to a husband who is my rock and generally (insert chuckle) loves me unconditionally despite all my faults. I have three beautiful children I will always love fiercely.

So, I put on my yoga pants every day, put my hair in a bun, write to you and run a little business/mission I am proud of. Being a mom might look different this year, but I am grateful for my blessings and the opportunity to be in this space called "now." I suspect there might be a time in my life I reflect back a bit fondly.

So, to all the other moms out there...do not try to do it all perfectly or be too hard on yourself...take more time to cherish the moments...and yourself. Be a hero for yourself today and always. A wise person in my life recently told me this...my mom.

EVEN IF YOU ARE EXHAUSTED, PRETEND TO BE STRONG AND HOPEFUL

This week, today, tonight...I am exhausted. Plain and simply exhausted. Today our daughter's anxiety was high, debilitation apparent. We had multiple care team consults and completed intake paperwork (including updates to our daughter's health timeline) to initiate a Neuropsych evaluation. This must be the 10th (or maybe 20th...I have lost count) intake/referral package my husband and I have tackled.

I am reminded tonight that our daughter's health timeline is powerful — it illustrates her journey and strength. It is in these moments of exhaustion and frustration that I need to pretend to be strong and hopeful...for our daughter, our children, my husband, and myself (hoping...daring myself...telling myself to believe it...embrace it). There is plain and simply no alternative.

The below timeline is shared to be informative and educational. We hope it might help another family feel not alone in their journey and feasibly something to be learned or considered that might help a loved one. The one thing I have learned about mental illness...is all the things we do not know.

Please Note: *The timeline has been updated throughout the writing of this book.*

Our Daughter's (Our Family's) Journey

9/16/20: Our daughter experienced acute anxiety and panic attack or panic-like event at well-child check in anticipation of vaccines.

I struggled to get our daughter out of the car and into the medical facility. She was hesitant and in tears. In the exam room, she suddenly demonstrated symptoms of a panic attack — something I had never witnessed. Butterflies in her stomach, dizziness, tingling in her hands, and loss of feeling or weakness in arms and legs. She settled down and received vaccines like a champ — flu shot, 1st HPV vaccine, Meningococcal MCV4, Tdap.

9/17: Our daughter called us from the dance studio — panic attack in restroom — asked us to come get her.

9/18: Pediatrician prescribed hydroxyzine and recommended counseling if symptoms did not improve in a few days. Stopped hydroxyzine after 24 hours — dropped our daughter's heart rate enough that she was scared and uncomfortable.

9/22: Daughter's symptoms were significantly worse — seeing some anxious trembling, combative behavior, and screaming. We called a nurse who recommended we take her to a local hospital. The hospital ran a variety of tests/bloodwork. Only red flag was irregular thyroid results, but was not conclusive or significantly alarming. They sent us home with a few doses of Ativan (lorazepam) to control elevated panic attacks and recommended we see her pediatrician. Social Worker recommended our daughter see a counselor immediately.

9/25: Pediatrician drew more blood for additional follow-up and started our daughter on fluoxetine. We completed our intake appointment with a counselor. Our daughter's symptoms continued to worsen. Symptoms had migrated from butterflies in her stomach to feelings more relatable to a heart attack — chest pain, shortness of breath, increased dizziness, weakness in arms and legs. She was becoming truly terrified and, as a result, increasingly frustrated, angry, and combative. She would say things like, "I cannot live like this. Make it stop. I will make it stop. I want to be with our dog in heaven."

9/29: Daughter's symptoms were so bad we no longer felt she or our family was safe. At the recommendation of the Washington County Crisis Hotline (Minnesota), we brought our daughter back to the hospital. At the hospital, she was deemed unsafe to be home and admitted. Recommended by social worker that she be medically cleared and transferred to inpatient mental health hospital.

Our daughter spent seven days in the hospital waiting for an inpatient mental health bed. Every day her symptoms got worse while we waited. The hospital stopped giving our daughter fluoxetine, thinking it may have contributed to her suicidal thoughts. The hospital attempted to show her some coping mechanisms for her anxiety, but her ability to control or regulate her sensory system continued to degrade. Only toward the end of our stay did hospital personnel agree tamping down or proactively treating our daughter's symptoms was necessary. My husband and I fought for answers challenging medical personnel to overturn every rock. At our encouragement (after already medically clearing her), doctor-on-call ordered an MRI, EEG, neurological exam, and psychiatric exam. MRI and EEG were never completed after the neurological exam.

Our daughter's symptoms worsened throughout the weekend. Panic attacks were lasting hours, and symptoms never went away — she had ongoing feelings of dizziness, shortness of breath, feeling life is not real, and chest pain — went to sleep with them and woke up with them. Constant urination. Hospital started collecting and testing urine. Noticed OCD behaviors — our daughter started picking at eyelashes and eyebrows. Becoming obsessed with candy and angry if not received.

In our daughter's worse moments, she would be screaming, pounding walls and windows, on the floor crying, combative to those helping her, and hitting herself. At one point on Sunday (10/4), we were asked to leave the room because she was so bad sedation or restraint were being considered.

10/5: Our daughter was transferred to a local youth inpatient mental health hospital by ambulance.

10/5 — 10/14: Our daughter's stay at a local inpatient mental health hospital. Guanfacine and sertraline (Zoloft) started. Her panic symptoms stabilized. Family requested her strep titers be tested and PANS or PANDAS be considered.

10/14: Our daughter came home. Happy and excited to be going home. Did not look well, but extreme behavior seemed stabilized.

10/14: Family learned of high-risk Covid exposure. Quarantined.

10/15 — 10/18: Our daughter hit a low state of depression. Wanted to see a nurse from local inpatient mental health hospital. Attempted to run away on multiple occasions to find nurse. Required constant supervision to keep safe.

10/18: Family tested for Covid. Learned we were negative.

10/19 – 10/23: Our daughter started at an intensive outpatient program or partial hospitalization. Psychiatrist suggested we test for PANDAS. Bloodwork scheduled for Friday (10/23). Our daughter was very depressed and angry this week. High anxiety, panic, and obsessive behaviors continue.

10/23: Our daughter mentioning she wants to die. More about not wanting to live like she is feeling and less about hating her life. Psychiatrist recommends she spends the weekend at local inpatient mental health hospital and a medication change from guanfacine to clonazepam. Medication change was a game-changer for her – an upper versus a depressor.

10/26: Our daughter is released from inpatient hospital.

10/28: Readmitted to IOP or partial hospitalization. ½ day program. Attempted school portion at home with school district.

10/28 – 11/23: Our daughter attended IOP or partial hospitalization. Headaches, dizziness, feelings of life not being real, and icky feeling in her stomach are consistent and continue. Advised either medication or psychosomatic symptoms. Continues to be obsessed about candy and urination. Picking eyebrows and eyelashes. Does not look well. Panic decreases a little, but generally, she does not feel well. She is trying hard to be better. Struggles to do school or dance. Both cause anxiety and panic.

11/3: MRI at local children's hospital.

11/4: Approximate date in which ten days of penicillin started – Strep Titers 231.

11/25: Road trip to Florida – a favorite place for our daughter

— hopeful it might bring her some peace and joy. Our daughter started five days of azithromycin. Her panic symptoms start to worsen significantly. Presenting almost seizure-like. Fisting of hands, face contorts, stuttering of words, loss of words, irrational thought, behavior that does not make sense. Overall noticed increasing immature behavior and reactions over last three months. Daughter as we knew her, rarely seen.

11/25 — 12/4: Daughter's symptoms continue to worsen. Always worse at night. Typically, mornings okay. After noon (or 12 pm), we notice she starts to degrade. By 3 pm, anxiety/panic becomes more possible. After 5 pm typical. 8 pm very typical. Fear, thinking she is going to die, life is not real, she is not real, we are not real, seizure-like attacks. Psychiatrist quadruples her clonazepam. We notice her behavior and overall feeling of "icky" worsen. We stop it on Wednesday (12/2). We substitute ibuprofen and notice it makes her feel better — helps headaches, dizziness, and overall feelings of ickiness. Does not completely control panic with one dose, but does help curtail it.

12/4: Daughter and I fly home from Florida. Our daughter flies without medicinal assistance.

12/8: See new medication manager who suggests again our daughter has PANS/PANDAS, and we schedule an appointment with PANS/PANDAS specialist. Suggests we start supplements such as fish oil, magnesium, L-theanine, inositol. We continue vitamin D3 — identified earlier she is vitamin D deficient.

12/13: Connected with a parent of a PANDAS child. Suggested we start regular doses of ibuprofen or anti-inflammatory to reduce swelling in the brain. Coupled ibuprofen every five hours with supplements mentioned above.

12/14: Connected with a provider that specializes in PANS/PANDAS. Suggested we start CBD and consider diet change. Scheduled appointment for 12/28.

12/17: Our pediatrician called to advise we continue an anti-inflammatory and start our daughter on 30 days of 250 mg/ml cephalexin, 10 mls, 3Xs a day.

12/18 — 12/22: Noticing CBD does not work as well as ibuprofen. Taking in most cases 2-3 capsules a day. In addition to all supplements, a dose of ibuprofen around 3 or 4 pm. But overall new regime has given us our daughter back — we see personality return; she looks better, and behavior improved a bit. Immature behavior continues, but overall, much more agreeable and helpful.

12/23 — 12/27: Our daughter's panic symptoms worsening again. Lots of fear and life is not real. Episodes can last 15-30 minutes. Episodes more frequent. Has complained of a sore throat over the last few days. No other symptoms.

12/28: Neuro Quant MRI, 19-channel qEEG brain mapping, extensive blood tests, and Cunningham Panel ordered by provider specializing in PANS/PANDAS.

12/31: Neuro Quant MRI and blood tests completed.

1/11/21: Follow-up appointment with provider specializing in PANS/PANDAS. Immune vulnerability could be a factor; the up-trending of strep antibodies is significant based on her symptoms. Specialist thinks there is an inflammatory, immune-based issue. Concerned about POTS. Per NeuroQuant MRI seeing inflammation and atrophy in the brain. Shows that our daughter's medial orbitofrontal is atrophied. This would indicate trouble with executive functioning, which parents have confirmed. The temporal pole is also atrophied on the right, more so than the left. This could indicate injury or infection in these areas of the brain. Cerebral gray matter, thalamus, putamen, pallidum, primary motor, inferior temporal, and supramarginal all are showing up as inflamed portions on her report. Histamines are high — nearly double average or normal. Strep, Parvovirus B19 IgG & IgM, and Coxsackie B antibodies high. IgG borderline deficient. Eosinophil Absolute is high. Specialist curious about Lyme disease and Mast cell activation. Cholesterol, zinc, and iron low. Additional medications/supplements added: zinc, Zyrtec, Super Milk Thistle, Meriva Curcumin, BioPure cocktail (for possible Lyme). Additional blood tests ordered.

1/19: Suggested by Children's Infectious Disease team that our daughter sees a specialist at a local university hospital. Our daughter's chart sent over for review.

1/21: Additional blood tests completed as ordered by provider specializing in PANS/PANDAS. Our daughter saw a neurologist for a 2nd opinion. Not familiar with a NeuroQuant MRI — not seeing inflammation and atrophy in the brain. Has ordered a Mayo Autoimmune Panel — suspected Autoimmune Encephalitis or Encephalopathy.

Month of January: Our daughter is back to her old self and fairly "normal"— 90% of the time. Cannot engage in anything school-related without panic attack. Has re-engaged and dancing again with her competitive team. Doctors, disagreements between siblings or with parents, "no," high anxiety/ stress moments cause a similar reaction or panic attack. Panic attacks are getting more violent. Look like a severe temper tantrum. Inability to control arms and legs. Hits herself and objects. Fear she may hurt herself or others trying to help her. Screams at top of lungs. Can last a couple of minutes to 30 minutes or an entire hour to calm her down. Nothing (medication or coping mechanisms) helps our daughter once escalated other than to hold/hug her or significant sensory change (i.e., bath). Impacting other children in the home — have to remove children from home when our daughter is having a bad episode.

Late January/early February 2021: Meeting with our daughter's mental health counselor and school counselors to discuss additional support needed for school. A 504 plan has been drafted. Parents requesting counseling for entire family, including younger siblings who do not understand — seeing anger, confusion, and tears.

1/31: Our daughter's anxiety and panic symptoms worsening. Started 5-day dose of prednisone. 20 mg dose 2x a day prescribed. 20 mg too much for our daughter. Gave 10 mg dose 2x a day or ½ dose for five days. Interrupted sleep. Panic and anxiety exacerbated.

2/1: Appointment with provider specializing in PANS/PANDAS to review most recent bloodwork. Our daughter prescribed valacyclovir 1-gram oral tablet, 1 tablet, 2 times a day for 30 days. New supplement added for suspected toxin exposure (N-acetyl-L-cysteine–NAC 900 mg, 1 capsule 3X a day). Raised concerns regarding increasing anxiety and panic. Asked to decrease medication/supplements. Little, if any, removed. Taking 22 items 1 — 3Xs a day.

2/1: Started raising concerns with counselor and medication manager regarding increasing anxiety and panic.

2/4: Our littlest has a sore throat and low-grade fever. Tested for strep and Covid — both were negative.

2/5: Last day of prednisone.

2/12: Family tested for Covid — negative.

Week of 2/14: Conversations with counseling team, Medica, and Washington County Crisis Team regarding concerns and severity of anxiety and panic. Concerned for our daughter's safety (injury during panic episodes and increasing "bad thoughts"). Considering day treatment programs. Cannot manage at home.

2/17: Our daughter taken to a university ER due to severity of panic attacks and safety concerns. Admitted for one night. Met with psychiatrist and infectious disease team. Team currently believes severe panic disorder. Questionable autoimmune encephalitis or PANS. Increasing sertraline (Zoloft) dosage to 75 mg and considering as much as 100-150 mg. Adding trazodone, 12.5 mg once a day...could be used twice a day. If it zonks her out — consider as an "as needed" option for panic. Recommending we stop all antibiotics/supplements to give her body a break. Not seeing benefit or change. Engage a psychiatrist and additional behavioral support. Canceled next appointment with provider specializing in PANS/PANDAS. Onboarding additional psychiatric and behavioral support.

3/1: Appointment with infectious disease doctor at university hospital. Recommended focus on behavior and psychiatric support and treatment.

3/2 to 4/27: Counseling increased to 2-3 times a week. Onboarded 2nd counseling team (equestrian life therapy and wellness coaching). Sertraline increased from 75 mg to 125 mg via 12.5 mg increments over the course of weeks. Noticed low blood sugar having significant impact on behavior/increased anxiety/jitters/dizziness — increased snacking to avoid what we assume is low blood sugar or impact of medication. No longer able to go to dance practices, but can attend dance competitions. Anxiety continues to be extremely debilitating. Continue to see behavior/intellectual/age regression.

4/28: Care counsel with our daughter's entire medical/behavioral team (case manager, behavioral counselors, med manager, pediatrician, and school counselor). Physical, vital check, gene testing, hormone testing, increased counseling, change in medication plan, EEG, and neuropsych evaluation discussed.

5/8: Pediatric appointment. Height (5'-0") and weight (83 lbs.) — growth normal. Great BMI. Appointment ended abruptly due to a panic attack.

5/10: Gene testing complete and reviewed. Recommended med change. Instead, adding anti-anxiety booster (buspirone, 5mg — increase to 10 mg daily) to 125 mg of sertraline to assure additional support onboard before making med change, not knowing efficacy of one or both.

5/11: Follow-up meeting with pediatrician. Suggested we prioritize neuropsych evaluation, additional psychiatric consults, and possible referral to Mayo.

5/12: Meeting with daughter's case manager. Advised our daughter's anxiety is acute and panic attacks severe. Situation and response unusual. Not a typical case. Need to consider medical reason for behavior/psychiatric changes again.

Early June: Increased buspirone to 15 mg a day. Added back anti-inflammatory (ibuprofen) every 6-8 hours and low dose of Augmentin (or Amoxicillin and clavulanate) 875-125 mg.

July: Began Exposure Therapy for Panic Disorder.

8/9: Mayo visit for Comprehensive Anxiety Evaluation with psychiatrist and psychologist. Confirmed Panic Disorder. Med plan generally supported. Increasing buspirone from 5 mg (3X a day) or 15 mg to 45 mg.

September 2021 — January 2022: Now taking 7.5 mg of buspirone 3X a day along with 125 mg of sertraline (1/2 in morning and 1/2 in the evening). Returned back to school (or 7th grade) after missing her entire 6th grade year. Quit dancing. Started chamber choir and drama club. Continued working with Exposure Therapy team and Equestrian Therapy team. Anxiety and panic remain high. Aggression greater now than when panic started. Team suggesting a re-evaluation of diagnosis and medications.

February 2022: Parents exhausted. Littlest (6-year-old daughter) begins counseling to address trauma she has experienced.

3/28: Meeting with Med Manager. Medication changes suggested. Replace 125 mg of sertraline with 75 mg of venlafaxine daily. Introduce 5 mg of propranolol 2x daily or as needed to manage anxiety. Medications titrated up and down over the course of a month. Eventually, we might stop 7.5 mg of buspirone 3X a day.

3/29: Meeting with pediatrician. Height 5'-0" and weight 100 lbs. No height change for nearly a year — something to be watched (follow-up appointment scheduled and possible bone scan if no change). Weight has significantly increased. Pediatrician wanting to run medication plan by resident psychiatrist.

3/31: Start new medication plan.

4/1: Pediatrician calls and recommends we pause medication changes per conversation with resident psychiatrist. Psychiatrist recommends 10 mg of citalopram 1X daily instead of 75 mg of venlafaxine daily. Consult between providers scheduled.

4/7: Our daughter starts new medication regime (10 -20 mg of citalopram, titrate down sertraline and continue 7.5 mg of buspirone 3X daily). Medication changes will take 4-6 weeks.

Our journey continues...

DON'T LET FEAR BLOCK YOUR BLESSINGS

Last night, my husband and I dreaded...feared...a conversation we needed to have with our daughter. We hated the idea of it so much, the potential panic attack, depression, and short/long-term impact, that we (not due to avoidance, but by design) waited as long as we could to have the conversation. Wouldn't you?

Parenting a mentally ill child is extremely difficult. You cannot unravel what is behavior, manipulation, hormone changes, or mental illness. Obviously, how you parent a given situation might look very different if it's behavior/manipulation versus an illness. Not knowing how to parent, you often wonder...and despite every best intention and love beyond measure...am I helping our child, harming our child, setting them up for success or failure coupled with a dose of depression? Where is that darn handbook for parenting, anyway? I know I asked earlier...has anyone found it yet?

So, back to last night...

We needed to address "dance." So, you might understand the significance of this conversation...our daughter has been dancing since she was three (she is now twelve). She may have danced before she walked. It has never been about how good she is or the number/size of trophies...dance is simply a part of who she is and what she does...making this conversation that much harder.

For reasons we do not and may never understand, our daughter has been able to dance competitively at competitions. However, she can no longer attend dance practices...in person or virtual, from home. What was a healing activity for her this past winter (following her hospitalization), has become a source of anxiety resulting in debilitating panic leading to the rare ability to attend and participate in dance practices. Watching your daughter fear something she loves...try to walk through the door of a studio and community she has felt grateful to be a part of...is beyond painful. And then hit the repeat button every week...at least twice...not easy for any of us. Simply confusing beyond measure.

I wish I could put into words how hard it is to watch your daughter be unable to do something she has naturally done for years...and not because she is physically unable (she is perfectly able...I have watched her when she thought no one was looking), but because her mind prevents her in anxious situations by throwing all her senses into fight-or-flight. I often watch our daughter cry as she tries to fight complete and utter debilitation. Her heart wants to dance, but her mind simply will not let her. She is literally trapped in her own body.

We sat our daughter down together (my husband and I). Yes, good parenting 101, but in reality, we needed the emotional support and were prepared for the physical reaction that might occur. We even went so far as to contact those our daughter might reach out to in a possible panic following our conversation to prepare them in advance. We advised our daughter that we felt it was best to pause dance and focus on healing. An opportunity to get really strong for the upcoming school year and dance season. (Back to that missing handbook...good advice for a healthy child...potentially unfair and harmful advice for an ill child.) News delivered...we braced ourselves...and waited.

Our daughter surprised us. She cried...sadly, and grate-fully she cried. Crying is a rational response. Crying means our daughter's mind was still online. In this rare and rational moment, our daughter reminded us how important dance is to her. That despite the irrational fear, she needed and wanted to attend practices to compete...to go to nationals in Texas this coming June. She pleaded with us to help her. So, despite our own exhaustion around watching our daughter struggle, we agreed to hold her hand while she valiantly faced her fears.

Why do I tell this story? I am learning every day how important it is to not let fear block our blessings...our dreams...our aspirations — for us and our children. I watch a young girl every day power through debilitating fear holding on with all her strength to who she is and whom she wants to be...rather than allowing herself to be held back by her illness today. I am not sure how this story will end or if she will make it to the national dance competition in Texas. But I do know, without a doubt, that our daughter is the strongest person I know.

ACCEPT THAT IT IS
OUTSIDE YOUR CONTROL

It is 1 am Saturday night/Sunday morning. I was tired...and asleep. Our daughter has been restless tonight and unable to sleep. She has finally settled. I now find myself watching her sleep...watching her chest rise and fall. Protecting her.... nine months later...from what...I am still confused. I gave up on sleep, rolled over, and turned on the light. Grabbed my laptop and started typing...so...here I am.

Our daughter had an amazing week! Probably the best since "before." I should be so grateful...relieved...even thrilled. And I am...truly...but in all honesty and full transparency...I am also still scared and hesitant.

As I watch our daughter sleep, I notice her coloring seems off. She does not have eyelashes (because she constantly picks them). Her sleep cycle is off, resulting in the use of 3-6 mg of melatonin a night to get her mind/body to settle/relax (well above the 0 mg of melatonin she used to take or the typical 1 mg dose most children might take). She takes 125 mg of sertraline a day along with 22.5 mg of buspirone to manage her anxiety/panic/depression (and honestly, we have no clue what is working or possibly hurting). We watch her diet differently and manage her day around meals to prevent low blood sugar (triggers her anxiety). She exhibits intellectual and age regression that sometimes can be both heartbreaking and challenging to parent.

So, yes, our daughter is doing better, and we are grateful. However, like any parent in this situation, I cannot help but wonder if we are masking something we have not properly diagnosed, with not one, but multiple medications. And who is "we?" My husband and I are playing a greater and more prominent role in diagnosing and treatment plans than any parent should or should need to. I cannot begin to describe how frustrating this is.

Recently our pediatrician suggested we consider a Neuropsych evaluation for our daughter. What is a Neuropsych evaluation? Still, to this day (despite our research and counsel with our daughter's team), we do not fully understand, but desperate to turn over every rock for our child, we moved forward with the referral. We proceeded with intake and another stack of papers to complete redundant to the stack we had just completed...and redundant to the stack of papers we completed before that. We completed our paperwork, mailed it in, and at the mercy of the "system," we waited for our phone call from "scheduling." "Scheduling" did call, thankfully, only a few days later. A "Team Meeting" was recommended for our daughter after reviewing her chart. It was explained that our appointment would be nearly three hours. One hour with a psychologist and one hour with a pediatrician, followed by a 30-minute summary of findings/recommendations with both psychologist and pediatrician in the same room. Halleluiah!! This is exactly the type of collective care, evaluation, and counsel my husband and I have been asking for since our daughter got sick. Sadly, for nine months, we did not know we needed to be seen by a Neuropsych team. We did not know who or what we should have been asking for.

My moment of relief was replaced with the continued

frustration most of us with a mentally ill child feel. The soonest our daughter could be seen was 6 months out with testing following this appointment. If we are lucky, we may have a summary of findings within 10 months...if we are lucky. In the meantime, our daughter waits, and we pray she continues to improve even though we continue to question her diagnosis. And aside from that, as I watch her sleep...I cannot help but wonder what good or harm we are doing.

So, forgive me, my husband, or any other family that journeys with a mentally ill child. We are tired, frustrated, and even angry. The current model of care needs improvement, alignment, and continuity of care versus fragmented specialization and disjointed delivery. Children's mental health needs visibility, an investment of resources, and prioritization.

WHAT WE SEE DEPENDS
ON WHAT WE LOOK FOR

It is happy hour at the lake...4 pm, Memorial Day weekend in Alexandria, MN. And although a happy hour does mean a glass of wine, possibly some appetizers, and a pontoon ride, today it simply and wonderfully means the sun is shining on the first weekend at the lake for our family in quite some time. My niece and nephews are playing in the water, and our younger kids are enjoying a quiet moment with me in a bedroom with big picture windows that overlook the lake. My husband is making pesto in the kitchen to serve with steak...a fan favorite for our littlest's 6th birthday party (yes, it is unicorn-themed, and our littlest daughter is wearing a unicorn costume complete with head, tail, and wings...all rainbow, of course.) A pretty blessed and beautiful moment... because it is ours... our happy place/space.

Not much has changed at the lake. A few repairs and adjustments one can expect when opening the lake home or cabin in the spring. Kids are a little taller, the dock might be leaning just a little more to the right, the pontoon is once again full of towels, and there is a new jet ski in the water. Generally, at this moment, all seems right and as it should be. I am grateful to be together and for the familiar sounds of people playing on the lake.

In this moment, it is easy to forget that an hour ago, our oldest daughter had a panic attack on the boat (suddenly forcing all of us back home) ...a very real and unwelcomed reminder that life has indeed changed for our family. But I am also finding that as our daughter starts to get a little stronger and "episodes" are, thankfully, farther apart (maybe days... even a week...rather than hours), I find myself a little more lost in purpose and direction...even feeling a little crazy for wanting/needing to protect her as I do. I have been living in this changed reality for a length of time now and uncomfortably finding myself a little confused/unsure how to move forward as some "normalcy" returns to our lives...and maybe for all of us (in some capacity) if you consider the impact and changes Covid has imposed on our lives and way of thinking.

But the funny thing (but actually not that funny at all) is that as soon as you feel a little more confident, a little more comfortable...possibly some peace in your life and let down your guard...your child that is a braving a mental illness suddenly and without warning is having a panic attack in the middle of the lake. You find yourself in a new situation (yet again) and racing the boat home because you are afraid of both the "what ifs" you have already experienced and feasibly jarring experience for her cousins. Gratefully today, our daughter's episode was short and less explosive than most.

The hard part for any family living with a child with a mental illness is that we do not know why or if our child is truly getting stronger. I am not sure our daughter will get better, but she and we may be learning to accept and live with/manage her anxiety and panic, resulting in fewer high stress/crisis situations. BUT she is heavily medicated, and we have removed all the triggers that cause her anxiety and panic. She cannot and does not attend school. She cannot and does not attend group dance practices. We cannot attend the children's museum or the zoo. Today, cold water and a go-kart race threw her into anxious moments, resulting in one panic attack and a near miss later in the day. She lives in a fairly safe and protective bubble...relatively okay 95% of the time. Would you consider our daughter better? I honestly do not know how to answer the question.

So, how to feel, what to believe, and how to simply "be," remain confusing but for different and changing reasons as we help our child and family navigate an evolving mental illness. I guess what we see depends on what we look for. I pray my husband and I are looking for the right things...our daughter's mental health and healing depends on what we see and communicate to those around her (be it doctors, family, friends... even strangers). It is hard when others are looking for something different. They cannot help what they see, and I cannot help feeling a bit lost in the discrepancy.

LET GO OF WHAT HAS PASSED

We are currently in Colorado visiting family and headed up into the mountains today for a night in Breckenridge. We had arrived only 30 minutes earlier before taking a short walk to the base of Peak 8 for lunch. After ten minutes, our daughter was in distress. Dizziness, upset stomach, numbness in limbs, trembling, weakness, and disorientation. She advised me she did not feel anxious or think of anything that might cause anxiety or panic. Instead, I watched as dizziness induced anxiety that was quickly evolving into a state of panic.

Not really knowing or understanding, it appeared that the high altitude triggered somatic symptoms caused by hypoxia (oxygen deficiency), such as breathlessness, heart palpitations, and dizziness. Most of the symptoms our daughter was feeling are identical to those she experiences during panic attacks or moments of severe anxiety. So, in this case, I believe the symptoms initiated by high altitude actually began to increase her anxiety, inducing panic and debilitation. It is also in these moments that we see age regression and/or executive functioning impairment.

Still, after so many months and more panic attacks than I care to count, I still do not know how to confidently parent escalated situations. In this particular case in the mountains, do I insist our child power through the high-altitude symptoms and watch as she struggles to stand or walk? Do I insist she needs to eat lunch and take the gamble that our child will not have a severe panic attack in public, resulting in additional intervention? Do I rush our daughter down the mountain to alleviate the high-altitude symptoms knowing it is a decision that will impact the day for an entire family? I honestly do not know the right answer and continue to be so frustrated by this.

I do not feel confident in my ability to parent our daughter. I might need to let go of what has passed to move forward. Meaning...protect our daughter a little less, so she can grow stronger and more confident in who she is today (versus holding onto who she was). Parent her more and more like I would our other children, trusting she can manage her anxiety and panic better than she could in the past. I look forward to tomorrow without the fear and uncertainty the past has caused, realizing the blessings and strength that have found us when not looking.

OWN IT &
BE PROUD OF WHO YOU ARE.
IT IS YOUR SUPERPOWER.

A note to our daughter...

Honey, over the last nine months, I have watched you struggle and grow. I think you are quite possibly one of the strongest people I know...wise beyond your years. I do believe your journey with mental health has taught you more than many of us can appreciate and understand...even at many years beyond your age. I hope despite all the challenges you have experienced in the last year, you someday reflect on the gift you have been given...your superpower...but let's catch the others up...

Two days ago, your dad and I made a difficult decision...a decision all three of us have worked so hard to avoid. The decision to pause dance and focus all our efforts on your mental health in an effort to get you back on the team this fall in bigger and better ways...to get you through those school doors in August for the first time since March of 2020 (or seventeen months). A decision that might appear insignificant to others, but your dad and I recognize dance is a part of who you are. We know how much you needed dance during a confusing and scary time in your life. It was your light...your connection to others when feeling lost and alone—your connection to a community and identity before you got sick...your safe space. We know, honey, how much this decision frustrates you. We are so sorry, but hope someday you understand the decision was a thoughtful one...a decision that involved many and evolved over months...a short-term loss for a long-term gain. But I get these words hold little weight and probably little meaning for all the loss you are experiencing/ have experienced in the last year.

You need to know how much stronger you are now than a month ago...three months ago...six months ago... Your tears, although difficult for your dad and me, are a sense of relief. Tears are a rational response to a loss (you did not panic). We held you as you cried...cried from all the depths of your little body for the last nine months. And then amazed us as you got up, wiped your tears, and accepted the decision. And then I watched/heard you do something well beyond your years...

I walked past your room the next day following our decision and heard you say to a friend, "Do not feel sorry for me. I do not want any pity. Pausing dance was a decision my parents and I made to focus on my mental health. I might miss one competition, but I will be on the team next year — I am determined to be even better and stronger. I have so many competitions to look forward to."

Now I cried...I cried because in the last nine months...

- *You braved three ER visits.*
- *Experienced three extended hospital stays (two at an inpatient mental health hospital).*
- *Admitted twice to an Intensive Out-Patient program.*
- *More medications than any child should ever need.*
- *Medical visits/conversations with more providers than I care to count.*
- *Missed your entire year of sixth grade.*

I shed tears because, despite ALL of the above, you are owning who you are and where you are at.

With pride,
Mom

TIME, FAITH, HOPE & LOVE

It is Sunday, Father's Day. My parents just left, our three children are playing (well, the littlest is at my feet, supposedly bored with "nothing to do"...despite a room full of toys), and I believe my husband is washing his car and the dog (let it be known I did not ask him to do either of these on Father's Day).

Our oldest daughter has been amazing...beyond amazing... personality, light, executive functioning, maturity, independence, returning more and more each day. I realize I feel genuinely good and at peace for the first time in a really long time. It hits me that, although I know my family is on a journey (we all are), it is gratefully and frustratingly true that time, faith, hope, and love can heal...but cannot be rushed.

I have a new hypothesis about our daughter's mental health and experience. It is a hypothesis, and I am not a medical professional. I am sharing my thoughts only as a reference or "something to consider" for other families/ individuals that might be experiencing/diagnosed with acute anxiety/severe panic disorder following a traumatic event or terrifying experience. Sadly, a hunch that might only make sense after we have ruled out so many other medical diagnoses following blood tests, psychological examinations, hospitalizations, physical exams, medications, supplements...etc.

As a reminder, our daughter experienced a panic attack at a well-child check. Prior to this event, there were no indicators of any underlying mental health conditions or illness. Our daughter's sensory system following this panic attack never relented...symptoms of fluttering/upset stomach, dizziness, feelings of being hot, racing heart, perceived shortness of breath, and loss of sensation in limbs all got progressively worse within two weeks. Our daughter was admitted to a local hospital and, for seven days, waited for a mental health bed. Her symptoms got progressively worse...terrifyingly worse... nearly resulting in sedation and restraint to calm her body, mind, and sensory system that was malfunctioning. From that moment on, our daughter was in-and-out of mental health hospitals for nearly two months and on various different psychotropic drugs that did not appear to do her any favors (despite best intentions). Medications made her feel worse (specifically increasing dizziness). Physical reactions resulting from medication(s) scared her, resulting in increased anxiety. It became a vicious cycle. The sicker our daughter felt... the greater her anxiety and the more severe and often her panic presented. I really believe her mind and body began to know only one way to function. It got stuck (of sorts)...anger, frustration, excitement, and sadness all started to look and present in the same way.

I wonder...if our daughter simply had a panic attack and if her physical symptoms had been managed differently...would we be where we are today? What we have seen from the beginning is that our daughter's panic is sometimes tripped by physical symptoms (those mentioned above) rather than simply acute anxiety. For example....we are seeing summer heat trip our daughter's anxiety. We have seen high altitude (dizziness and shortness of breath) scare our daughter into a panic attack. We have seen physical exertion or activities (i.e., dancing and running) raise our daughter's blood pressure, resulting in elevated anxiety. I am starting to believe more and more that our daughter needs to learn how to regain control and manage her body's sensory system — disassociate physical symptoms from anxiety. In some cases, it is when our daughter cannot escape or control her physical symptoms, panic occurs. So, after so many months, I sometimes wonder if we are dealing with a sensory system disorder rather than simply anxiety and panic disorder. I know they are related, but should we be thinking a bit differently?

In addition, there are some who believe anti-inflammatories and antibiotics can help those that experience anxiety. After months of trying any and all methods (including these), I do not believe these are necessarily "treating" anything, but instead preventing illness or feelings/physical symptoms of being ill (i.e., headache or a fever), that can be associated with anxiety. Again, by calming the body...keeping the body quiet and calm...you calm the mind.

Our daughter's inability to participate in larger group activities suddenly makes more sense. Despite her desire to participate in things like dance, the zoo, or children's museum (and tears that prove she desires to participate and mourns the loss), she often talks about it being too loud, too much commotion, scared of how she might feel...all preventing her from participating and being far from parents for the "just in case." I do not believe she has anxiety about large group activities. Rather, the physical symptoms she associates with a panic attack create anxiety or avoidance. Panic attacks are terrifying — she naturally and protectively avoids any situations that might trip her physical symptoms — we all would.

With this change in thinking or reframing, we have quieted her life. We started to peel back some of the medications and are slowly reintroducing our daughter to smaller/quieter activities. We are focusing on building back confidence and not fearing natural physical symptoms. Every day our daughter gets stronger, and the idea of returning to bigger things gets a little easier to consider.

MOVE BEYOND WHATEVER LIMITS LIFE PLACED ON YOU

A friend said something to me earlier this week...something that stays with me and causes me to pause...often. She said, "Kristin, your daughter is not going to 'get past' her mental illness." And like a few others in my life, I think she was gently saying that I need to accept where our daughter is at, who she is now, and how that will continue to impact our lives moving forward. I continue to tell others around me I have accepted our journey, but honestly, I am not sure I have. In full transparency, I continue to wait for the "miracle" that will reset the life we used to have. However, truth be told...I am not sure I can or want to go back either...I am not the same person...we are not the same family.

I am reading the book *Limitless* by Mallory Weggemann (a Paralympic gold medalist). Her introductory words resonate deeply and occupy our thoughts. They have created a bit of turmoil in my mind and heart this week, but I recognize the need for the struggle and courage to move past the idea that we are going to "get past." I share some of her writing with you below. For those that journey with me...it will hit home. For those on a different journey, I am confident you will find strength and wisdom in her words.

Mallory starts, "Quick fixes and neat resolutions aren't always realistic." Wait...does the author know I am a type A firstborn? Quick and neat is who I am. She goes on to say, "Challenges may knock us flat again and again, odds may be stacked dizzyingly high against us, and the world can seem so wildly unfair that we are tempted to give up. But life is about the long game, and what seems overwhelming in the moment could very well be pointing us toward something greater. It's up to us to push past the noise of our present, past expectations placed upon us, and into the boundless possibilities of our unwritten future."

"We have no way of knowing where the future will take us...we just have to trust that there is something beautiful waiting for us." Mallory continues, "It's like the quote often attributed to Marin Luther King Jr., 'Faith is taking the first step even when you don't see the whole staircase.'" Although Mallory is referencing a physical disability, I wonder if she knows how much her words mean to those braving a mental illness.

Mallory continues, "I never dreamed I would find more meaning and freedom in life *because* of my struggles. I have shed the restrictions placed on me — by others as well as myself — and built a life rooted in possibility, potential and promise. When I refused to accept limits to what I could do, I threw open the door to a life that's bigger and fuller than I could ever have imagined."

She goes on to say, "It's not about naïve optimism; it's about believing in the power of resilience — the combination of courage, passion, patience, and perseverance — to create something meaningful out of difficult circumstances. Resilience is simply doing what you have to do for as long as it takes. You don't have to do it with grace, and you don't have to do it with cheerfulness — you just have to do it. It's simultaneously that simple and that profoundly difficult. It's also the only way to move beyond whatever limits life may have placed on you." I sometimes feel silly for holding onto hope so tightly, and this need to be positive (despite daily doses of anger and frustration)...this idea of naïve optimism. I often tell others and our daughter...what choice do we have?

The author adds a final thought to her introductory note, "When we remove every boundary that hems us in — physical, emotional or societal — we become limitless. When we reject preconceived notions about what something 'should' look like, we move ourselves toward the possible. The real secret to overcoming setbacks is developing the wisdom to know which goals are worth pursuing and which weights — expectations, limitations, and disappointments — we must let go to rise to the top. Don't be afraid to cut anchor. Fight your way back to the surface."

From Mallory and others in my life who quietly and patiently guide, coach, and love me, I am learning that there isn't really such a thing as going back to "normal" after trauma or tragedy. You cannot go back because somewhere along the way, your perception of normal changes based on your experience. Life for me...for our daughter...for our family...is still limitless. It will just be different...and with time, I will fully accept this...maybe even embrace it.

THE ONLY WAY IS THROUGH

We are engaging a master-level psychotherapist this week that specializes in the treatment of panic disorder/PTSD. He utilizes Exposure and Response Prevention therapy (ERP). His goal...to teach our daughter not to be afraid of her panic or the physical symptoms associated with panic. This does not mean avoiding a panic attack...this means teaching her not to be afraid of the panic attacks she most certainly will have. The approach is graduated. Eventually, with time the mind and body are retrained or reprogrammed to not be afraid. Panic attacks go away or decrease enough to allow "normal" and healthy function. But I am not going to lie or sugar coat it...we most likely have an uncomfortable month or few ahead of us...then we tackle the aftermath of the last year and potentially irreversible consequences.

There is simply no other option anymore...around it does not work...the only way is through. Every day we tell our daughter to be brave...we pray she/we have the courage to beat this disorder that has rocked our world. And once beat (whatever "beat" looks like)...we then begin the journey of learning how to live with the different path paved...regardless if we wanted to take it. We are on it, and there is no going back.

"EVERYTHING I HAVE LEARNED ABOUT LIFE: IT GOES ON."

A quote from Robert Frost, "In three words I can sum up everything I've learned about life: it goes on."

I am not talking about the obvious resilience and fortitude needed when caring for a child or loved one that has fallen ill...these characteristics are a given...there is no other way. I am talking about the undeniable need for resilience and fortitude in the space of taking care of "you." As I weigh the decision or need to go back to work...honestly and openly...I am hesitant. I am nervous for the obvious reasons centered around wanting to be available for our children and a desire not to fill my plate too full again. I also recognize and accept that I am a better person, wife, and mom when I am not balancing a full-time career with the demands at home. But...what really weighs heavy on my heart...I am proud of who I am now and what I have accomplished during a time of adversity. I have never felt more centered and grounded in who I am and my purpose. The thought of "going back" feels like an unwelcome surrender to the comforts I once knew during a time I struggled with identity and self-worth. "Going back" feels like the opposite of resilience and fortitude when I have fought so hard on so many fronts over the last year.

For nearly a year, I have slowly and intentionally molded a very different life than the one I lived prior to our daughter's first indication of a panic disorder. Most of the work was quietly done at night when our daughter and family slept. Days were centered around care...and at times...survival. But, while my family slept/sleeps, I have built a business, began to write, started speaking, and became an advocate for change and a community leader.

I share all of this as a reminder for myself. A reminder for when life throws me another curve ball...and it will...that surrendering to the uncertainty does not provide strength. I share this with the reader as a reminder to take care of "you" when taking care of a loved one. It is possible and okay to keep living even when in a crisis or in a space that feels uncomfortable. It might take a little more effort, a bit more time, lots of self-care, diligence, and determination. Frankly, some days you might feel a little self-centered (and even ridiculous at times) for investing in yourself while someone you love struggles. But what you need to know and trust...you are a far better care provider when you are taking care of your physical, mental, and emotional well-being.

Life marches on...it always will. We cannot control the deck we are dealt, but we do get to choose how we play the cards. Remember...we are playing the long game. Life always goes on...and so must we.

Continue living.

STRENGTH OF LOVE, IMPORTANCE OF FAMILY, AND NEVER GIVE UP

I reflect back to when our oldest daughter struggled most. There were times my husband and I had to ask our nine-year-old son to take his five-year-old sister into her bedroom. He knew to grab a movie and headphones and to close the door to avoid the unwelcome sounds and sights of the panic attacks that plagued our oldest. I cannot begin to describe how that felt as a parent recognizing the insanity of the ask and horrible reason for the ask.

In addition, I remember tears from our littlest every time we took her sister to a medical appointment. Tears that stemmed from our eldest's second ER visit resulting in a transfer to a local inpatient mental health hospital. Our littlest never got to say "goodbye" to her older sister and waited seventeen days to see her again. Every time our oldest experienced a panic attack, it induced fear in our littlest around the possibility that her sister would be "taken" and not come home. I remember being in the throes of keeping our oldest daughter safe while my heart broke for our other two children, lost in the chaos of it all. Experiencing things...being asked to do things...seeing and hearing things you would never wish for any child.

Our son is our middle child and only boy. Always a little lost in the shuffle or understanding how and where he fits in a household full of girls. While we were not watching this past winter, our son found his independence and thrived in the space of trust and growing respect that happens with age. Under the guidance and care of an admirable 4th-grade teacher, our son flourished as a virtual learner. He learned responsibility, practiced time management, and began to understand the importance of commitment and the consequence resulting from the failure to keep a commitment (a good lesson learned). Early this spring, our son was asked by a soccer coach during a casual recreational practice to join the traveling U10 soccer team. Keep in mind our son was nine, so asked to not only play on a team but one year beyond his age. I am saddened to this day that I did not see this ask coming...and somehow still surprised by it today. I simply was not as present as I wanted to be in our son's life...should have been...and wished with all my heart I could have been. Our son is our only boy and will always have a special place in our hearts. I will forever admire his compassionate heart and wisdom beyond his years.... he teaches me something new every day.

Our littlest girl, or our third, is our survivor. Maybe as a parent, I should feel bad about this, but honestly, as a first-born, I am proud, and a bit envious, of this quality. Our littlest is independent, strong-willed, and confident. I cannot tell you how many times I have found her in the fridge (because we failed to feed her in time (according to her)), on the counter (because she needed to wash her hands, but no one was helping) or suddenly reading a book (because she taught her herself to read...tired of waiting for us). She is six years old and has "goals," ...according to her. Our daughter was born happy...with a sense of humor...blue eyes...and curly blonde hair. Cute and funny...she quickly learned she could get away with just about anything. Gratefully a trait that did not "go south" but instead created a determination and sense of "can do" I am proud of. Now she wants to be a dancer...like her big sister. I am grateful our darling little girl still wants to be like her big sister. Thankful for the countless handmade cards with rainbows, flowers, and unicorns gifted out of love and hope her big sister would be well enough to play with her again.

So, to our littlest children...

I love you! I am so proud of your strength and resilience during a difficult time. But, most importantly, you never stopped loving your sister or believing in who she was, even when you may have gone days, weeks, or months without seeing the sister you knew or understood. I will forever be sad for the lost time and not being as present as every mom and dad wants to be, but grateful for the independence and confidence learned...because you had to. These qualities will serve you well in the future. Do not forget the importance of unconditional love and faith in a person. I hope someday you forget the scary and confusing moments, but forever appreciate the strength of love, importance of family, and to never give up on someone you care about. I am sorry for how you had to learn these lessons, but forever grateful you did at a much younger age than most. Now you are even more special than you already are...if that is even possible.

DANCERS WHO LOVE TO DANCE ARE SO BEAUTIFUL TO WATCH

I have been crying for two hours. And many of you might feel my tears are unnecessary and the situation is undeserving. But, for others that have similar journeys, I know you understand I have no control over the emotions that have overcome me. I learned earlier tonight that our oldest daughter made her dance team. Gosh, such a simple statement...seemingly not important (maybe even ridiculous)...really insignificant in the grand schemes of what is important or should be important in life. But, for our daughter...dance is her world. You take away dance, and suddenly there is a loss of friends, pride, joy, and expression of who she is. Dance is our daughter's art. It is her way of expressing who she is and what she feels in a safe way. Dance has been her lifeline and her fuel. It is her community of friends and teachers...her strength and courage.

For many, it might appear our daughter never tried out for the team...but "magically made it." She never set foot in the studio that all the others practiced in for two weeks and bravely auditioned behind closed doors. But our oldest did something truly admirable for a child battling an illness that has left her with debilitating symptoms and uncertainty about who she is and how to confidently proceed. Despite all odds (and without thinking, but instead simply feeling with a heart fueled by passion), she choreographed her own dances by genre and submitted them to her teachers. My husband and I never made a suggestion...never even hinted...we were not even aware until we stumbled upon our daughter in the basement quietly auditioning in the only way she could. She was alone, on her own terms, and in a quiet setting, she could control. Not because this is how she actually wanted to audition, but the only way her body and mind would allow her.

I reflect back on being a 7th-grade girl...age twelve. I have always prided myself on being fairly confident, headstrong (well, my husband and parents would say I still am...not always a positive comment...laughs) and driven. But honestly, I am not sure I would have had half the courage and determination I see our oldest daughter demonstrate every day despite her fear, anger, frustration, and disappointment as a result of her unwelcomed panic disorder.

Our daughter has to face her panic disorder head-on...the only way is through. She works every day...chipping away at it...exposing her body to activities that induce the physical symptoms that cause her panic and pain. Think about that for a second. Our daughter walks "toward the fire" every day despite fear and physical/mental discomfort. In the last couple of weeks, she has battled through various panic attacks to walk through her dance studio doors, determined to get back on that dance floor. Maybe only appearing to be five minutes for some, but our journey started in the morning and did not end until she went to sleep. Managing through a panic disorder is not simply about the panic event itself. There is preparation, actual panic event, and feelings of sadness and loss following an event.

We recognize that there is still so much mountain to climb, and nothing is for certain. But for a moment, our daughter has been given hope and purpose...and for that...I am beyond grateful.

ALMOST ONE YEAR LATER, THE STRONGER VERSION OF ME

I want you to hear from our daughter. Nearly one year later, she asked to tell her story and share what she learned...in her voice...not mine. So, I asked her the following questions. I have edited responses only a little, so please accept the authentic nature of the writing.

What has been the hardest thing to understand as it relates to your mental health?

I changed from "normal" (a word we no longer often use in our home) to someone with a severe panic disorder over the course of a few days. I am confused about why my body and mind will no longer let me do things I could so easily do in the past. My panic disorder sometimes will not let me go to dance (for example). I LOVE dance. I cannot always control my body's physical reactions, which are often different from how I feel. It can be so frustrating and overwhelming. I literally cannot control my behavior or my body's physical responses... I am often embarrassed and understand my behavior is not always okay. I often end up in tears. Not being able to control your body and your feelings is frightening. Most people do not understand or can relate to the irrational nature of it all. I know they were and are trying to help me. I often feel like I am letting others down and being judged for behavior that is not mine but instead the result of my illness. I work hard every day, determined to conquer this disorder. I hope others see that I am trying...I am trying so hard every day.

How have you had to change?

I have had to change my daily routines. I approach activities differently. I used to go to dance (for example) with little thought or care. I was excited and could go easily. Now I am nervous. I am not nervous about dancing. I am nervous about what my body will do/feel and having a panic attack. There are more steps, and I start prepping my mind and body hours in advance.

Also, I dislike surprises. Surprises make me nervous. But, knowing too far in advance is not always good either — I might think about it too much, and my body will react in ways I cannot control. So, my parents are learning how and when to tell me things.

In addition, I always have to have a plan and take my medication in advance. These are tools that help me control my body's automatic responses to being nervous. My plan for dance, for example, starts with a special song my mom and I play in the car on the way to dance. I like my mom to be visible while I am dancing. If I need her, I know she is there, but more often, knowing there is someone around that understands my panic disorder simply helps me keep my body and mind calm. I wear earplugs to quiet the studio music and voices — loud noises and chaos trigger my anxiety and panic. We have hand signals like baseball players. If I touch my nose, my mom knows I am okay. If I touch my ear, it means I am getting nervous. This means she just needs to stay close while I try to power through my anxiety. If I need a quiet moment, we step out of the dance studio together. I calm my mind and body and go back in. Giving up is no longer an option. I am working hard to retrain my body and mind.

How have your relationships changed? Do you feel they have changed?

I do not feel as connected with my friends right now. I lost a year, and they kept moving forward. They are at a different time and place than me. Sometimes I cannot relate. I know with time, this will change, but it is really hard right now. I sometimes feel lonely.

I do not know anyone in school. I missed my entire 6th-grade year...it feels overwhelming...especially as I look at returning to school in a couple of weeks.

My anxiety and panic can sometimes cause me to say or do things I am embarrassed by or not proud of. Sometimes I might walk away from a person or situation to manage my anxiety and panic. People often do not understand this and get frustrated with me. I wish I could tell everyone to have patience with me and to forgive me. I am learning to change some negative behavior my panic disorder has caused. I just want to be who I was before all of this...but in some ways... there are things I have learned that I am proud of.

Also, as far as my family — I feel closer to my mom and dad. My mom and dad have told me so many stories to help me through hard moments. I feel like I know them better than I did before. Crazy to think of my parents as kids like me...chuckles.

What have you learned?

To not take things for granted. Your life can change so quickly. Do not focus on the bad or hard things in your life. Be grateful for and appreciate all the good things.

Has it taught you to appreciate other things/people differently?

I now know what it feels like to feel "different" and have a disability or something that can be disabling in some situations. My tolerance for friends/family/people treating others unkindly or unfairly is low. My mom tells me this is one of my superpowers, and it makes me feel strong. I often will say something or step in to help. I am not shy because I know how it feels to have something you cannot control or choose to have. I know how those being unfairly mistreated feel. I want to be a voice for them.

And I guess...despite the really hard year...a year I never want to repeat...one year later...I do know I am a stronger version of myself.

WALK FORWARD
WITH CONFIDENCE

I am often asked, "How did you do it?" My answer is simple. "You just do." You cannot live in fear, you cannot worry about all the "what-ifs." You certainly need a great deal of faith and trust in the ones you love. Now, I am not going to pretend that I live with our daughter's mental illness gracefully (my husband and parents would disagree). But, the one thing I can say with confidence based on our experience...somehow, you always find a way. Whatever your "way" is...embrace it, own it, love it and steer it. Put the "what-ifs" in your back pocket and walk forward.

THE ANNIVERSARY OF SEPTEMBER 16, 2020

The anniversary of September 16, 2020, or the day that changed our life, is just a few days away...The day our oldest experienced her first panic attack that transcended into an ugly panic disorder that sent our life into a tailspin we did not know how to pull out of. I wonder how the day will feel...I wonder if I will notice...I wonder if our daughter, husband, or children will notice.

Our daughter has returned to 7th grade and dances again. There are certainly reminders almost every day that her panic disorder lurks in the shadows, but we are hopeful we know how to keep it there. Most importantly...our daughter is no longer ashamed or embarrassed by her mental illness...often mentioning it in conversation if the context justifies the reason for her changed or thoughtful (often mature beyond her years) perspective.

Our family had to summit a mountain before healing could begin. We had to overturn every rock to be ready to accept the simple truth that our daughter had a panic disorder. She had a mental illness, not induced by an infectious disease, but instead something she might live with for the rest of her life. Like many parents, I think we hoped for a "reason" and quick fix or "a fix." We had to rule out everything before we were ready to accept the truth. In addition, hindered by PTSD as a result of early hospitalization, traditional and clinical approaches did not work for our daughter. Our approach had to and continues to look, feel and be different.

We surrounded ourselves with a strong, diverse, and comprehensive mental and physical healthcare team. A team that was both right for our daughter and our family. A team that included our county crisis team, a medication manager, equestrian therapists, exposure therapists, a pediatric team that did not give up, insurance partners that removed roadblocks to care, our daughter's compassionate dance studio, and school counselors/administrators that cared beyond the call of duty. A team that surrounded our daughter and family 2-3 times a week this past year, working with her in our home, her dance studio, and at her school. The team met her where she needed them most (both physically and mentally). Rather than avoiding anxiety/panic attacks, our daughter and family learned to shoulder them, plan for them, and accept that the only way was through (not around or avoidance). We learned not to be afraid, and slowly, over time, we watched our daughter's panic disorder recede into more manageable emotions and behavior.

Finding the "right" team took us time with many partners along the way that steered and supported us. Finding the right team was not easy...and then layer in months of waiting "to be seen" in a healthcare system that is under-resourced and overwhelmed. In addition, mental health is unpredictable. Trying to predict care needed now or in the future is a gamble, so the thought of decreasing care or moving forward without a team at any time is unsettling. We live with knowing there is another child and family that waits and might need our care team more. We know because one year ago...that family was us.

KNOW WHAT YOU WANT...
AND SHOW UP

Monday night, our daughter had a panic attack at dance. We anticipated last week would be hard. The first week of "the reality of the year." School is now in full swing, the new dance season has started, and generally, the whole family is busier and schedules fuller. There is not as much time to find peace, quiet...and opportunity to regroup self and emotions. Something necessary for our daughter's mental/emotional health...I think many of us would say the same.

Monday night (or dance) started with tears and frustration. I am sure our daughter felt overwhelmed. Dance is a lot for young girls. Practice is typically 3-4 nights a week and often 4-5 hours long. Seems like a lot for a child? Yes, many of us would agree. But, balance that with less time for social media, positive, healthy friendships, physical exercise, and an opportunity to be a part of a team, the alternative (not being involved) is less desirable and frankly scary.

Our daughter's initial reaction Monday night was to quit dance. She is battling a lot of demons from last year...a great deal of loss. In regard to dance, she lost a year of practice. She is currently in the process of regaining strength, flexibility, and technique. She is more than grateful for making the team and understands the gift she was given, but it's also difficult for her to watch her former teammates progress forward while she repeats. We have all been there and can empathize. The feelings and frustration are real, and despite knowing that being angry at "unfair circumstances outside our control" is not productive, they still show up. For our daughter, when they show up...they show up BIG. The physical symptoms associated with feelings of frustration, sadness, or anger can trip her panic. Sadly, a normal reaction transitions into what feels abnormal or irrational. Add in hormones and simply the awkward stage of being a 7th-grade girl...heck, she is handling it with more grace than I probably could/would in my forties...and certainly better than I could at her age. But sadly, it does not always present that way.

We continue to tell our daughter the only way is through. She will have to work twice as hard as anyone else in many aspects of her life...not just dance. Yes, last year was unfair, and we are not sure "why her." But we tell her she cannot go back, dwell on the past or even hope to be the girl she once was...she can only go forward.

The following day or Tuesday, our daughter had her first pointe class. A huge milestone for our daughter, who has been wearing ballet slippers since she was three. But, unlike her friends, she was pre-pointe...they had new pointe shoes, and she was still in her ballet shoes. Darn, the obvious visual reminder of difference.

LET IT COME. LET IT BE. LET IT GO.

Today I need to let it be and simply just "be." The week was a mix of wonderful moments and some really hard moments. Today, I set aside all work and responsibilities at home to simply be with our family. I do not want to think about what was, what could have been, what should be, what I do not know...I plain and simply want to be. To be here in this moment with our family simply because we can. I am not thinking about tomorrow or all the things I should be or could be doing. I simply need a second to take a deep breath with those I love.

Today I will...Let it come. Let it be. Just let it go.

YOUR GREATNESS
WON'T LOOK LIKE THEIRS

Last week was hard. Our daughter swirled a little with the anniversary of her hospitalization upon us. Change of colors, fall scents, pumpkin bread, pictures of then and now...all reminders that her life is changed...a life she did not choose, but now lives. In addition, she had a bad cold. Aside from all the struggles of simply having a cold during a pandemic, being sick for someone suffering from acute anxiety only exasperates things. It is a trigger or reminder "something is not right," elevating stress and anxiety. Any interruption in schedule or routine (i.e., being sent home from school due to illness/ missed dance) triggered feelings or fear that "it" (meaning our daughter's onset of her panic disorder/three weeks of hospitalization) is happening all over again. Events initiated multiple panic attacks, exhaustion for parents, and reminders (again) that we do not know how to parent this despite one year of "training." And reality/truth...there is no "training," and every day might present something new or unexpected. Second "truth"...this is also called "parenting." And third "truth" ...parenting a pre-teen during a pandemic, social unrest, age of social media (and then layer on that panic disorder) is REALLY hard! My husband and I...despite highest and best intentions...fail every day.

For the last year, our daughter has been told to be courageous. To be honest about how she is feeling...how a situation might make her feel. Aside from the good practice of always being honest about how we are feeling, something we all might strive to be better at, advice was and continues to be a coping mechanism. Again, our daughter cannot carry emotional burdens or stress that others may be able to carry. It is not something I necessarily understand or expect others to understand, but it is the reality of her mental illness. Something I have had to learn to accept and have patience with. However, it has taught me to exercise greater patience and compassion with others, recognizing we all approach situations and stress/anxiety differently. There is really no "right" or "same" way. Like everything else in life, we all manage stress and anxiety differently...and that is okay.

In addition, our daughter knows what it feels like to struggle every day. She quietly beats down a panic disorder... every second of every day...often in silence and alone, to protect herself and those around her. For others, struggles might be color of skin, gender identification, a physical disability, a demographic...the list goes on. She has very little patience for insensitive actions or words. Her emotional awareness and intelligence far exceed mine and most, so there are days that I struggle with, "do I applaud her behavior or correct it?" And who is the teacher? Me or her?

I am proud of our daughter...for her courage, awareness, honesty, and desire to address challenges head-on. I am learning from her...sometimes I wonder if I am learning more from her than she is learning from me. But she is twelve and growing/learning/making mistakes...like each of us (despite our age)...every day. We talk about harnessing our "greatness." We discuss how to best deliver a message - the right words to use, best ways and times to have a conversation, and how words might make others feel. We talk about bringing others along, accepting truth and reality, moving on, the importance of "how you show up", and so much in life is outside our control. I tell our daughter, "Your greatness won't look like theirs. That does not mean you are any less great." She reminds me to look for greatness in others.

WHICH VERSION DO YOU SEE?

As our daughter's new reality back in the "real world" unfolds, I watch her show up differently to different people. My initial reaction was to queue up her counseling team...and I did...we meet in a week to evaluate her treatment plan, next steps, and timeline. But, in reality, I am not so sure how our daughter is showing up in different circumstances is actually related to her mental health. It might simply be a preteen girl trying to figure out how to navigate a life that is a little less protected (and certainly a great deal more confusing) than the year before. For the majority of women reading this, I would bet most would say the preteen years might be the phase of life we collectively never want to do over—a time when belonging and feeling accepted outweighs just about anything else.

In one aspect of our daughter's life, she is flourishing! The situation is new, and those around her are new. She is learning, surrounded by friends, and seeking different opportunities that surprise her dad and me every day. Generally, she is energized and willing/wanting to be challenged. She advocates for children's mental health, she challenges all of us not to forget the children in the hospital via some philanthropic work, her awareness and compassion for others are off the charts, and this week she starts media training to prepare her for children's mental health advocacy work in the public sector.

In another aspect of our daughter's life, she is struggling, and her behavior is drastically different. In this space, she is reminded every day that she is different...her life unfairly changed. We see more significant age regression, regressed executive function, and memory impairment (disassociation). She is lonely, and her performance is declining. She is often in tears and angry at the situation, which sadly influences how she presents to and treats others. All of the above is not an excuse (and something we are parenting)...just the reality of the situation...loneliness inducing anxiety and frustration.

My personality and nature are often too quick to judge or even just perceive what I think or want to see. I might more often than I should see our daughter and others in the second light I describe above. Instead, I might need to examine myself. I am working hard every day to change that, and generally, I feel our world needs to do the same. We are all so quick to assume less than positive or good intent. So, I ask you...which version/circumstance do you see?...and does that perception influence what you see and how you respond? I, for one, have a great deal of work to do.

THE BEACH TEACHES US...

Today I sit on a beach in Sanibel, Florida...the same beach that just one year ago we brought our oldest daughter to, hoping her "happy place" might bring her (still undiagnosed) panic disorder some reprieve. I recall pacing on this very beach just 365 days earlier, begging her mental health providers on the phone for help and clarity...something to help rationalize the terrifying turn of events in our life.

Then and now...

The beach teaches that just because you can't see the sun in your life, it is still there. You must take it on faith. Each sunrise represents a fresh start and a new opportunity — to conceive and pursue a dream, to help someone, or to reach out for help.

EMPOWER YOUR STORY

Family and friends often thank us for our youth mental health advocacy work. They use words like strong, courageous, and inspiring. Our family is truly grateful for all the love, care, support, and encouragement. But, truth be told, we tell our story to heal...for us...and the hope along the way is that our story might benefit others. We tell it to feel empowered and strong during a time in our lives that can often be heart-breaking, confusing, and frustrating.

The Executive Director of NAMI Minnesota said something in a recent media interview we participated in that has stuck with me. She said, "The word 'stigma' is being moved away from — it too easily rolls off the tongue." (I reflect back on all the times I have used the word simply because others use it.) She continues, "What people are afraid of is feeling discriminated against. It is not about the person feeling shame for their condition or situation; it is our reaction to it that causes them to feel shame." Sue nailed it.

We do not tell our story for recognition, accolades, or for any other perceived gain. We do not even tell our story to reduce stigmas...per se. We tell our story to normalize the conversation, educate others, and reduce the shaming that occurs to ultimately alleviate the shame those with a mental illness (an illness they did not choose) feel as a result of our behavior/perception/misunderstanding/lack of education.

Our daughter never felt shame for her mental illness until others indicated she should. We have always empowered our daughter to tell her story...to be a voice for others...but just as important...to feel strength and empowerment for her own mental health and well-being. To feel some level of control in a space of life that can feel uncontrollable and extremely unfair. Our reaction to her and others that might appear "different" has to change. She is not a hero or "different"...we are not heroes or "different." We are simply trying to empower our family to be stronger than the shame that knocks at our door every day. And if our job as parents — to empower and protect our children benefits others — we are beyond grateful the additional value is gained.

Embrace and empower the story (whatever the story) — do not judge it. Listen and seek to understand. It is only then that real change and productive work/healing begins. The alternative...well, we simply cannot fathom living in a place of fear and shame. We will not...and neither will our children.

PERFECTION IS ACCEPTING THIS MOMENT EXACTLY HOW IT IS

I look in the mirror and wonder sometimes how, why, and when my life took a right turn. Like so many firstborns (that blame their parents for all our idiosyncrasies — sorry, mom and dad), I diligently handcrafted the life I wanted. Funny thing (and something you can only learn with time)...I now realize I was never in control of "the plan." Life unfolds chapter by chapter, and different from a book, you cannot skip to the last page to know how the story ends. Some might say knowing the ending ruins the book. Others (like myself) might argue that knowing the outcome does not make the story less enjoyable, but instead, there is comfort in knowing (what is typically) a happy ending.

When our oldest fell ill, life changed overnight. There was no foreshadowing or indication a change in our story was coming. We did not have that luxury. And just as quickly, I had to let go of who I was/who we were and accept who I/we are now. The future yet again remains unpredictable. I am learning to be okay with this...still not very good at it. But I hang tight to the hope and faith that all things happen for a reason. Really...what choice do I have? What choice do all of us have?

I am learning that a life of perfection is paved with disappointment. I am learning to enjoy the messy and imperfection of the journey, knowing my story/our story is still being written.

I remind myself every day not to miss the beauty found in the struggles many of us shoulder. Perfection is not something to strive for but instead, accepting this moment exactly how it is. Sometimes the unexpected moments can be a greater gift than the one(s) you planned for.

YOU CAN BE
ANYTHING YOU WANT

Diversity...equity...and inclusion (DEI). Words that mean something much different to me this year than this time last year. Only one year later, and yet I reflect on how much my perspective has changed, supporting a child that has limitations I never grew up with.

This past week I participated in a DEI class. I struggle with the idea that we need a class to remind us how to treat others humanly (above and before anything), recognizing our background and unique characteristics define our beautiful individuality. Sadly, we do not always cherish and celebrate these wonderful characteristics that make each of us unique.

We participated in a powerful exercise in which the entire class (local business/community leaders) stood in a long straight line...fairly equal in accomplishment. We were then asked questions such as, "Were you told you could be anything? Did you ever wonder when you would eat next? Were your parents graduates of college? Have you ever felt discriminated against or made to feel less than others? Have you ever received financial assistance or an inheritance from your parents?...etc." For every question that was an "advantage," we took a step forward. For every question that was a "disadvantage," we took a step back. Powerfully...only a few of us in the entire class of 30 never took a step back. A few of us took a number of steps forward with every advantage we were bestowed growing up. We grew up privileged and many steps ahead of our peers simply because we were born into a fortunate situation. Many of our peers today started a number of steps behind us and had to work twice as hard to accomplish the same goals. Now, this does not mean that everyone in the room did/does not work hard. It simply means those of us in the room born into greater privilege had additional means and support – a starting advantage and fewer roadblocks or hurdles.

Our oldest daughter is growing up with these same privileges...and maybe even a few more, surrounded by a community of family and friends with generous means. She has been provided every opportunity/means of support available to a child living with a mental illness. She is fortunate to have a diagnosis, a family that can afford medical care and counseling, a community that has wrapped themselves around her, a school team that is working hard to assure she is learning/set up for success, and parents that will tell her the same thing we heard growing up, "You can be anything you want."

But she may face discrimination and some challenges my husband and I never experienced. If she had been standing in "that line" with me...she would be a couple of steps behind me. As a mom/parent who wants nothing more than to see our children flourish, this is a hard realization. Our daughter is unique or different from most...or is she? Aren't we all different? Sadly, I now know, like so many others, she will unfairly experience discrimination or judgment. I know because she already has. Through our own circumstances/learned behavior, we each have our own bias... some of these biases we are not even aware of...affecting how we treat and approach others every day. I have my own...I am not sure it is even possible not to. But I remind myself to approach others with kindness and respect, recognizing that we are all people first. It is simple... really.

So, my ask...Remember to treat everyone "humanly" first and foremost. Celebrate individuality and learn from each other. If you want to know more or seek to understand...ask questions. Approach everyone believing they have the highest and best intentions...despite the optics of the situation. Remind every child (despite age...5 or 95) that they can be anything they want when they grow up. That they can do anything. Help clear the runway and let them soar.

IT IS OKAY…

It is okay to say, "I cannot, I need a break, or I need help." Yes…it is okay. It does not mean you or I are weak or uncaring. I am learning a great deal about the strength and courage needed to identify when help or change is needed.

Monday is a new chapter…or a different one. I return to work both with excitement and hesitation. Our daughter struggles, so I hold my breath and call for help. At some point, there is no choice but to move on…life requires it. I suspect I will not do this gracefully, but I will do it the best I can, surrounded by those that love our family. I hope our daughter is capable of transitioning with me…for her…for me…for us. As much as she might need my help…I also need hers.

DO NOT BE AFRAID
OF ALLOWING THE UNKNOWN

The best-laid plans can and will take a "right turn"...and then a "left." But regardless of if we are steering the ship or the current is taking us in a direction we did not anticipate, we need to trust all things happen for a reason. Do not let who we are today define who we need to be tomorrow. Life is unpredictable at best. It is how we embrace it that counts. There are certainly parts of the "former" me I miss. And, I wish more than anything, our daughter did not struggle and/or I could burden her pain. But I challenge all of us to not be afraid of allowing the unknown. Embrace the life that might be different despite fear, hardship, and challenges. In my case, I have found even greater joy and pride. It is no longer my resume that matters; but instead, it is the quality of my life, the well-being of our children/family, and a legacy I can be proud of. Never will I let fear or shame stand in the way...and neither should you.

I WILL NEVER GIVE UP

I wish I could say I was good at "this." "This" meaning parenting a child with a mental illness.

I wish I knew how to help our daughter. But, so many months later, I still do not always know how.

Others who struggle reach out to me for advice and guidance. Sadly, even after working with more providers than I care to count, I still do not know how to advise them.

Our daughter needs me. Often, I still do not know how to be there for her, although I am the one she calls for.

I am often exhausted. But I still do not give up.

I do not always know, but I am confident I will never give up on our daughter.

BELIEVE IN THOSE YOU LOVE

This past week our daughter struggled...to the point her dad and I were again desperate for intervention and help, initiating multiple conversations with her care team. BUT ALSO...our daughter soared, and you cannot help but wonder if you are overreacting or "what is wrong with me?" Mental illness is a constant roller coaster and not necessarily a ride someone, or a family can simply exit. One does not "get better," but instead, they (and those they love) learn how to cope and manage. It is an illness that impacts the entire family...not simply an individual. Sometimes you are in the first car of the roller coaster, scared to death, eyes closed and holding your breath. Other times you are in the back with arms thrown up, eyes wide, and feeling triumphant. Often the family is never in the same car...some okay...some struggling.

This past week our daughter's care team began over-turning every rock again (I cannot tell you how exhausting this repeated process is)—questioning if we are truly dealing with a simple panic disorder or if there are other physical contributors like a glandular disorder, malfunctioning thyroid or serotonin syndrome. You spend the week questioning what you know or trust to be true (again). You hear things like "at risk of being removed from home," "intensive in-home family treatment plan," and unidentified disorders that might be counter-acting treatment (despite that you have already done more bloodwork and testing than any young girl should have to endure). You spend the week first compiling a list of psychiatrists (because a list does not readily exist) and begin calling, only to learn most are not accepting new patients or first appointments are six to nine months out. You cannot help but feel frustrated and angry, wishing sometimes it would be easier if your child had cancer because at least then they would not have to wait nearly a year for a diagnosis or treatment plan. Chemo appointments would not be canceled because of viral exposures or snowstorms. And let's be clear — both cancer and mental illness are life-threatening. Situations like this leave a family desperate, exhausted, and living in a place of constant worry...for your child that struggles, yourself, your marriage, and other children.

But because answers are not readily found or available, you hold your breath, and you wonder where you will find the strength to continue navigating an illness so misunderstood, even by the professionals. A mental healthcare system that has truly never been built and is grossly under-resourced. You pull your family close and realize that strength is found by believing in those you love and trusting the strength of family. If we cannot find the team needed, we will build it.

"FIXING IT" IS NOT OUR JOB

Our beautiful daughter is standing 6 inches from my face... screaming at me. In these moments, it is difficult to see the beauty I know exists. I struggle to break free from her irrational anger, hurtful words, and need to cling to my body. I beg our daughter to stop...but, truth be told, I am not and will not beg. I instead work really hard to keep my cool, channel patience that wanes every week, and exercise the words/tools I have been taught by more counselors than I care to count. If it appears I am begging, it is simply because I am exhausted by an illness that is and will remain relentless. Our uninvited guest certainly has no intentions of packing its bags soon, regardless of how many times we have politely dropped a hint. Maybe it is time not to be so polite.

The physical discomfort of the moment will pass. It always passes. It is the emotional damage I worry about. Our youngest daughter cries and pleads with me, "to do something... Mom, fix it. Make it stop." Our son quietly retreats to his room and into his devices. How can I not feel like a failure? And darn it, I think I am starting to feel resentment toward our oldest daughter and the situation we have been in for eighteen months. And...shoot...now...I feel guilt for feeling resentment toward our child. A few days after peace and calm,

I will analyze the situation, question my recollection/response and wonder if there might be something wrong with me. It is an exhausting and vicious cycle.

But instead of relenting, I will continue to stand my ground and teach our children through our own actions the importance and value of self-preservation, perseverance, and accountability. I will remind them that we do not lean on the excuse, we do not sit in it, and we certainly do not give up or give in expecting others to fix it. Yes, I can continue to let our daughter...our children...our family lean into the disease (or mental illness)...an excuse...or I can push us into and past the discomfort. It is only if my husband and I model it will our children learn, value, and trust their own strength and perseverance. Sadly, as much as all parents might want to or wish we could, "fixing it" is not our job. But...always and forever...teaching is and will be.

MY CINDERELLA MOMENT

Last night was a night of celebration. A time with friends to pause, come together, and "just be" after nearly or over (I have lost count) two years of navigating Covid and battling a mental illness. So, how did I find myself in a cold car (alone, exhausted, and scared) at 11 pm on the icy roads of Minnesota, driving away from the warm and joyous celebration we helped host?

I reflect on the Cinderella-like moment. For one night, I hoped to set all our worries aside...the reality of our life...and don a gown and pearls. No, it was not a ballgown; it was a flapper dress. And no, I did not arrive by horse and carriage, but I did arrive with feathers in my hair and a heart that was full and happy. We attended a 1920s soiree benefitting youth mental health initiatives in Minnesota schools...discreetly our story was referenced, but not so discreetly, because I shed a few tears at the table. You would think after so much time, I would get used to our changed life, but reminders that we are different are still painful.

When the clock struck 10 pm, we learned our oldest daughter did not have her medication — unfortunately a medication that cannot be skipped. (Our children were staying with family in a cabin an hour west.) In addition, we learned our daughter was hiding under her bed, trying to escape the relentless and irrational panic disorder/separation anxiety that plagues her mind and body. Via text messages we were copied on, we saw our middle child (our ten-year-old son) begging his oldest sister to be okay (reminding her she is okay), asking if he could come sit with her, and pleading with her, "be strong for mom and dad." Our hearts broke. Gratefully, we learned our youngest was sleeping — we thanked our lucky stars for that one small blessing and additional heartache saved.

As a mom (or parent), I had no choice — I put my yoga pants back on, and with feathers in my hair, I jumped in the car and made the cold lonely drive while friends and family gathered. I did not cry until the next morning after the exhaustion passed and loss was felt. A loss that is so complex I cannot begin to describe. I cried alone only for a minute — anything longer is simply too exhausting and wasted effort. I shed just enough tears so the cup did not spill over. I gathered up my dress and feathers, wrangled the kids, and drove home. I reminded myself that I might just find my destiny on the roads I never thought I would travel — a turn that is intentional but destination unknown. I hold tight to the faith that this must be true and, with time, will forgive and forget yet another loss. Someday I will wear those feathers again, and hopefully alongside my daughters and on the arms of my husband and son.

CHOOSE LOVE OVER FEAR

My husband and I reflected last night on how much our family has adapted how we live with our eldest daughter. A choice? Not necessarily. Instead, a change that quietly took hold while we may or may not have been paying attention. Supporting a child with a mental illness is not something you do for a defined time period. It becomes your new way of life...you adapt to survive....a necessary change to live in a suddenly modified reality.

I have said it before but will say it again, "mental illness does not simply impact the one diagnosed." Our position and advocacy for some time has been reminding others that it also impacts the family...reminding providers and partners not to forget the parents in the lobby who are exhausted, out of patience/resources, and whose hearts are most likely broken. And, not to forget siblings at home who may have just endured an explosive situation and do not understand why their older sister was taken abruptly from their home. And, maybe the grandparents that quietly offer support however they can... exhausted with worry for both their children and grandchildren.

With time and the additional challenges and complexities we face, we are learning it is not just the patient or family...it impacts the entire network or community that engages with our family in any and all ways. Imagine a drop of dye in a glass of water. First, the impact of that dye is small and concentrated. It is much easier to protect our daughter, our family, our lifestyle, and shield others around us (to protect them as well as us). But with time, that dye slowly expands out (we have no control over it), impacting so much and many more. First, it was our extended family and close friends, then co-workers and neighbors...now strangers.

Our fear was that the further removed the impact is from our immediate family, sadly (but understandably), care, tolerance, and patience would be much less...misunderstanding and assumptions much greater, resulting in increased fear and shame. Amazingly, this has not been the case. Almost everyone who has been impacted by our daughter's mental illness has shown and continues to show our family love and support. A gift we are beyond grateful for and a reminder to do the same for others. Always choose love over fear.

FINDING ME...
FINDING YOU...
FINDING US...

Dear Daughter,

We say goodbye to the past and step into the present...the future knocks at the door.

Reflecting back, I now realize that the last year may have been about "finding me" to help you "find you." Yes, I realize that sounds a little self-centered, but let me continue.

While what I thought was a mom helping her daughter find her way in a new way...may have been the exact opposite. Another gift you quietly bestowed upon me this past year. Maybe you realized before I did that only after I found peace and comfort in our changed life could I truly be there for you. And it was hard...still is. But I now realize how much I needed to learn, and still need to learn, to be the mom you need me to be. I realize more than any other time in my life how messy and unfair life can be, but also the beauty and strength only we can discover if we choose to. And do not be fooled — I am no expert, and this will be ongoing work...never perfect. That is just the way life is...messy and always changing.

But now...I need you to "find you." This is not something I can do for you, despite all my efforts and desire to shoulder the burden. You have to do this on your own. That is my learning... my realization...and gift to you. Those you love will support you, be your cheerleaders, provide you with the tools, and hold you accountable to both your dreams and mistakes. Listen and respect them as their love is unconditional. But they cannot "find you" for you. This is something you have to do. Your road might be a little tougher than most, and I recognize that feels unfair. Yes, you can be mad, but what does that gain you?

Darling, you are lost right now and letting an illness control you. Yes, living with a mental illness is a roller coaster, frustrating and exhausting. I get it. We have some good days, and we have some bad days. It is not about "getting better." It is about getting "stronger." I am scared too, but I have seen your strength, courage, and determination — your accomplishments, despite an illness, are many. Yes, you might be different today than you were a year ago, but so are the rest of us. You are not unique. This, again, is called life. It is what you choose to do with the life you have and who you are today that counts. It will define you as you move forward. I need you to look in the mirror and see the same beautiful, strong, and courageous girl I see. Do not shy away from her — she is going to do amazing things. Do not give up on her, as I will never give up on you. But I do need you to "find you" and embrace her. Only then will you start to truly heal and embrace the person you are meant to be...not who you were.

Love,
Mom

CLOSING AUTHOR'S NOTE

I reflect a bit on where we have been, where we are now, and where we are headed. Truth be told, the only question I can answer (as described in the book) is where we have been.

Mental illness is rarely rational or predictable. You cannot rationalize something that is irrational, nor can I advise how our daughter's illness might present this afternoon, tomorrow, or a year from now. Nearly two years later, from the initial onset, our daughter continues to brave a severe panic disorder...this does not make us experts or heroes...it simply means we understand.

We understand you and the challenging journey your family is on. We know you desperately search for answers, treatment, and a miracle for your child or adolescent. Our family understands the exhaustion felt by simply trying to protect your loved one every hour of every day from both themselves and others who might shame them. We recognize how frustrating the questions that do not have any answers are or the need of others to rationalize something we have learned to accept (not because we understand), but because we must move forward and continue living. We know how alone you feel (despite a community of friends and family) simply because mental illness is so misunderstood...even by the experts we desperately pray have answers.

But despite all the challenges, trust we are all strong and empowered to make a difference. We are empowered to make a difference and influence change...for our child...for our family...for us. Similarly, empower your child to be proud, strong, and compassionate. Leave shame at the door — it does not have a place here...never has...never will.

Find comfort and strength in knowing you are not alone, and neither is your loved one. We are standing beside you, even though you might not know us or see us. Life always goes on...and collectively...so must we.

Together, we will be the force of change that is so desperately needed for all that brave a mental illness.

REFERENCES

Weggemann, M. (2021). *Limitless: The Power of Hope and Resilience to Overcome Circumstance.* Nashville, TN: Thomas Nelson

Dr. Seuss. (2022, Jan 21). in Wikipedia. en.wikipedia.org/wiki/Dr. Seuss

Robert Frost, (1874-1963). American poet

ABOUT ATMOSPHERE PRESS

Atmosphere Press is an independent, full-service publisher for excellent books in all genres and for all audiences. Learn more about what we do at atmospherepress.com.

We encourage you to check out some of Atmosphere's latest releases, which are available at Amazon.com and via order from your local bookstore:

The Great Unfixables, by Neil Taylor

Soused at the Manor House, by Brian Crawford

Portal or Hole: Meditations on Art, Religion, Race And The Pandemic, by Pamela M. Connell

A Walk Through the Wilderness, by Dan Conger

The House at 104: Memoir of a Childhood, by Anne Hegnauer

A Short History of Newton Hall, Chester, by Chris Fozzard

Serial Love: When Happily Ever After... Isn't, by Kathy Kay

Sit-Ins, Drive-Ins and Uncle Sam, by Bill Slawter

Black Water and Tulips, by Sara Mansfield Taber

Walking with Fay: My Mother's Uncharted Path into Dementia, by Carolyn Testa

FLAWED HOUSES of FOUR SEASONS, by James Morris

Word for New Weddings, by David Glusker and Thom Blackstone

It's Really All about Collaboration and Creativity! A Textbook and Self-Study Guide for the Instrumental Music Ensemble Conductor, by John F. Colson

A Life of Obstructions, by Rob Penfield

Troubled Skies Over Quaker Hill: A Search for the Truth, by Lessie Auletti

My Northeast Passage — Hope, Hassles and Danes, by Frances Terry Fischer

ABOUT THE AUTHOR

Hilda Berdie Photography

Kristin Rohman Rehkamp lives with her husband and three children in Lake Elmo, Minnesota. She currently owns and operates La Vie Est Belle, LLC (**lavieestbelle.live**); a brand that inspires giving and beautiful living. Given her personal experience with her oldest daughter, she is passionate about serving communities, organizations, and individuals working to break down barriers, raise awareness and make a difference in the lives of those braving mental illness.

Kristin proudly serves as a PrairieCare Fund Board Member and in various St. Croix Valley, Minnesota community leadership roles and programs. As Kristin advocates for her daughter through writing and speaking engagements, she looks forward to evolving mental health/well-being thinking and care models for those that journey with her family.

La Vie

EST BELLE

CPSIA information can be obtained
at www.ICGtesting.com
Printed in the USA
BVHW040329161122
651985BV00013B/1255